I0488870

Groundwater Depletion in the United States (1900–2008)

By Leonard F. Konikow

Scientific Investigations Report 2013–5079

U.S. Department of the Interior
U.S. Geological Survey

U.S. Department of the Interior
SALLY JEWELL, Secretary

U.S. Geological Survey
Suzette M. Kimball, Acting Director

U.S. Geological Survey, Reston, Virginia: 2013

For more information on the USGS—the Federal source for science about the Earth, its natural and living resources, natural hazards, and the environment, visit *http://www.usgs.gov or call 1–888–ASK–USGS.*

For an overview of USGS information products, including maps, imagery, and publications,
visit *http://www.usgs.gov/pubprod*

To order this and other USGS information products, visit *http://store.usgs.gov*

Suggested citation:
Konikow, L.F., 2013, Groundwater depletion in the United States (1900–2008): U.S. Geological Survey Scientific Investigations Report 2013–5079, 63 p., *http://pubs.usgs.gov/sir/2013/5079.*

Contents

Figures

Tables

Conversion Factors

Inch/Pound to SI

Multiply	By	To obtain
foot (ft)	0.3048	meter (m)
acre-foot (acre-ft)	1,233	cubic meter (m^3)
cubic foot per second (ft^3/s)	0.02832	cubic meter per second (m^3/s)

SI to Inch/Pound

Multiply	By	To obtain
Length		
millimeter (mm)	0.03937	inch (in)
centimeter (cm)	0.03281	foot (ft)
meter (m)	3.2808	foot (ft)
kilometer (km)	0.6214	mile (mi)
Area		
square kilometer (km^2)	0.3861	square mile (mi^2)
Volume		
cubic meter (m^3)	35.315	cubic feet (ft^3)
cubic kilometer (km^3)	0.2399	cubic mile (mi^3)
cubic kilometer (km^3)	810,713	acre-feet (ac-ft)
Flow rate		
millimeter per year (mm/yr)	0.03937	inches per year (in/yr)
centimeter per year (cm/yr)	0.03281	feet per year (ft/yr)
meter per year (m/yr)	3.2808	feet per year (ft/yr)
cubic meter per second (m^3/s)	35.315	cubic foot per second (ft^3/s)
cubic meter per day (m^3/d)	35.315	cubic foot per day (ft^3/d)
cubic kilometer per year (km^3/yr)	723.75	Billion gallons per year (Ggal/yr)
cubic kilometer per year (km^3/yr)	1,119.8	cubic foot per second (ft^3/s)

Groundwater Depletion in the United States (1900–2008)

By Leonard F. Konikow

Abstract

A natural consequence of groundwater withdrawals is the removal of water from subsurface storage, but the overall rates and magnitude of groundwater depletion in the United States are not well characterized. This study evaluates long-term cumulative depletion volumes in 40 separate aquifers or areas and one land use category in the United States, bringing together information from the literature and from new analyses. Depletion is directly calculated using calibrated groundwater models, analytical approaches, or volumetric budget analyses for multiple aquifer systems. Estimated groundwater depletion in the United States during 1900–2008 totals approximately 1,000 cubic kilometers (km^3). Furthermore, the rate of groundwater depletion has increased markedly since about 1950, with maximum rates occurring during the most recent period (2000–2008) when the depletion rate averaged almost 25 km^3 per year (compared to 9.2 km^3 per year averaged over the 1900–2008 timeframe).

Introduction

Water budgets form the foundation of informed water management strategies, including design of water supply infrastructure and assessment of water needs of ecosystems (Healy and others, 2007). As part of assessing water budgets, periodic assessments of changes in aquifer storage should be undertaken (U.S. Geological Survey, 2002). Groundwater depletion, herein defined as a reduction in the volume of groundwater in storage in the subsurface, not only can have negative impacts on water supply, but also can lead to land subsidence, reductions in surface-water flows and spring discharges, and loss of wetlands (Bartolino and Cunningham, 2003; Konikow and Kendy, 2005). Although groundwater depletion is rarely assessed and poorly documented, it is becoming recognized as an increasingly serious global problem that threatens sustainability of water supplies (for example, Schwartz and Ibaraki, 2011). Large cumulative long-term groundwater depletion also contributes directly to sea-level rise (Konikow, 2011) and may contribute indirectly to regional relative sea-level rise as a result of land subsidence issues.

Groundwater withdrawals in the United States have increased dramatically during the 20th century—more than doubling from 1950 through 1975 (Hutson and others, 2004). As noted by Konikow and Kendy (2005), groundwater depletion is the inevitable and natural consequence of withdrawing water from an aquifer. In a classic paper describing the source of water derived from wells, Theis (1940) clarified that withdrawals are balanced by some combination of removal of groundwater from storage (depletion), increases in recharge, and/or decreases in groundwater discharge. Furthermore, over time, the fraction of pumpage derived from storage will generally decrease as a system approaches a new equilibrium condition (for example, see Alley and others, 1999, fig. 14).

In estimating the contribution of long-term groundwater depletion to sea-level rise, Konikow (2011) estimated long-term groundwater depletion in the United States on the basis of analyses of 40 individual aquifer systems and (or) subareas that were integrated into the overall estimate (fig. 1), plus one broader diffuse land use category (agricultural and land drainage where the water table has been permanently lowered). For each system, area, or category, the 20th century depletion (1900–2000), the additional depletion through 2008, and the rate of depletion (1900–2008) were calculated.

The goal of the individual assessments in Konikow (2011) is to estimate the cumulative long-term change in the volume of groundwater stored in the subsurface. It is not intended to capture changes related to seasonal variations and (or) short-term climatic fluctuations. The purposes of this report are (1) to document the magnitude and trends in long-term groundwater depletion in the United States, and (2) to provide additional background information and details that support the methods and calculations used to estimate groundwater depletion for the 40 areas and 1 land use category of depletion in the United States—information that underlies the assessments in Konikow (2011). Because no substantial volumetric groundwater depletion is evident in Alaska, that area is excluded from the maps in this report.

Acknowledgments

E.A. Achey, S.M. Feeney, D.P. McGinnis, and J.J. Donovan assisted with analyses and calculations for some of the aquifer systems. U.S. Geological Survey colleagues G.N. Delin, D.L. Galloway, E.L. Kuniansky, and R.A. Sheets pro-

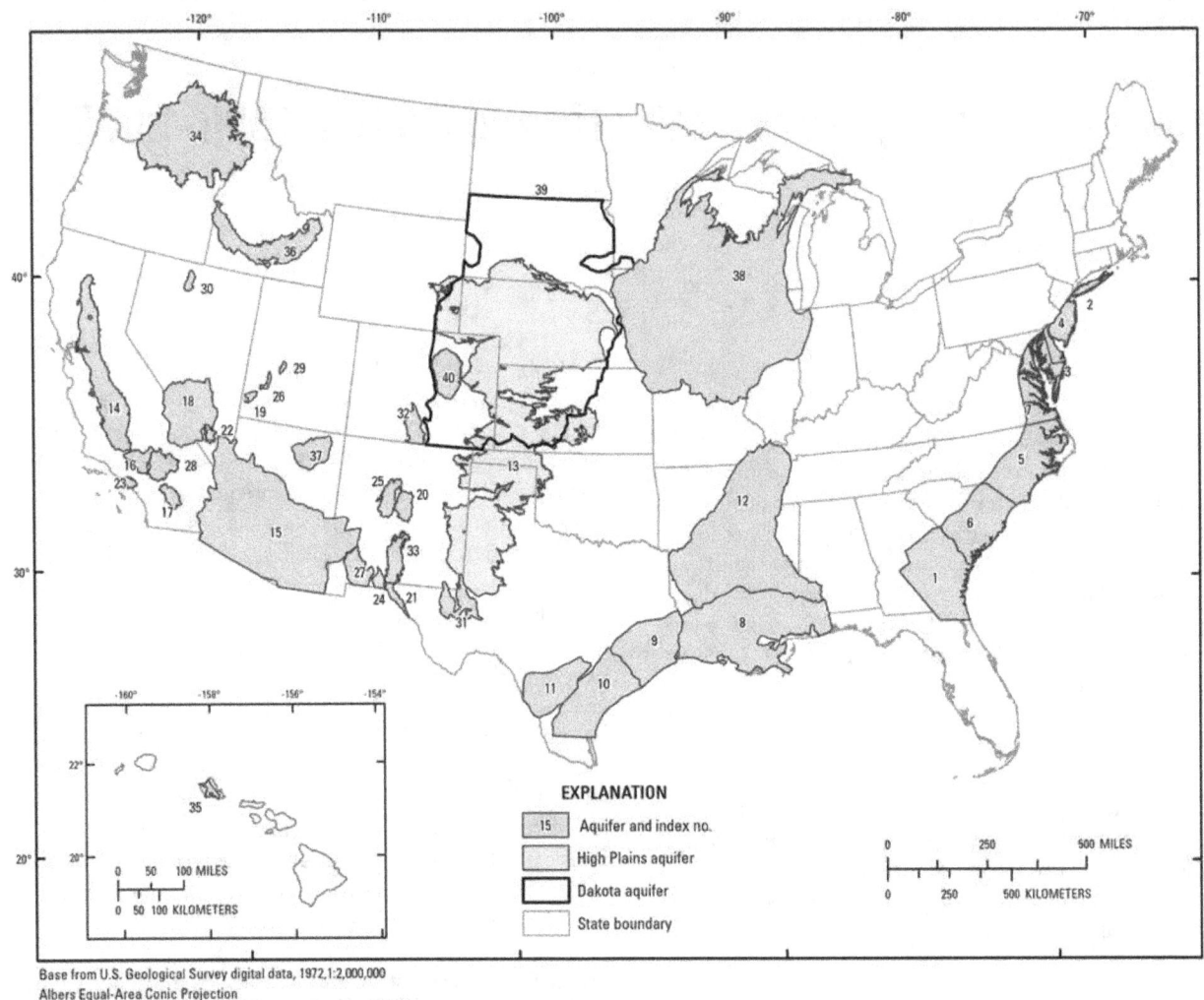

Base from U.S. Geological Survey digital data, 1972,1:2,000,000
Albers Equal-Area Conic Projection
Standard parallels 29° 30' N and 45° 30' N, central meridian 96° 00' W

Figure 1.   Map of the United States (excluding Alaska) showing the location and extent of 40 aquifer systems or subareas in which long-term groundwater depletion is assessed, 1900–2008. Index numbers are defined and aquifers are identified in table 1.

vided helpful review comments. D.J. Ackerman, E.R. Banta, J.R. Bartolino, L.M. Bexfield, J.B. Blainey, B.G. Campbell, A.H. Chowdhury, B.R. Clark, J.S. Clarke, J.B. Czarnecki, R.B. Dinicola, J.R. Eggleston, C.C. Faunt, R.T. Hanson, R.E. Heimlich, C.E. Heywood, G.F. Huff, S.K. Izuka, L.E. Jones, S.C. Kahle, M.C. Kasmarek, Eloise Kendy, A.D. Konieczki, A.L. Kontis, S.A. Leake, Angel Martin, Jr., J.L. Mason, D.P. McAda, E.R. McFarland, V.L. McGuire, Jack Monti, Jr., D.S. Oki, S.S. Paschke, G.A. Pavelis, D.F. Payne, M.D. Petkewich, J.P. Pope, C.L. Stamos-Pfeiffer, G.P. Stanton, S.A. Thiros, F.D. Tillman, B.E. Thomas, and J.J. Vaccaro kindly provided information about computer simulations, model results, depletion analyses, and (or) review comments for specific areas. S.A. Hoffman provided valuable assistance with Geographic Information System (GIS) tools and map preparation. This work was supported in part by funding from the U.S. Geological Survey's Office of Groundwater and the Groundwater Resources Program.

Methods

One or more methods were applied to specific aquifer systems, subareas, or categories to estimate the net long-term depletion in each system. These methods (numbered for cross referencing in table 1) included:

1. **Water-level change and storativity**: Integrate measurements of changes in groundwater levels over time and area, combined with estimates of storativity (specific yield for unconfined aquifers or storage coefficient for confined systems), to estimate the change in the volume of water stored in the pore spaces of the aquifer (for example, McGuire and others, 2003).

2. **Gravity**: Estimate large-scale water loss from gravity changes over time as measured by GRACE satellite data (for example, Famiglietti and others, 2011).

3. **Flow model**: Use calculations of changes in volume of stored water made using a deterministic groundwater-flow model calibrated to long-term observations of heads and parameter estimates for the system (for example, Faunt and others, 2009b).

4. **Confining unit**: Apply the method of Konikow and Neuzil (2007), which requires estimates of specific storage and thickness of the confining unit, as well as head changes in the adjacent aquifer, to estimate the depletion from confining units. For confined aquifer systems, leakage out of adjacent low-permeability confining units may be the principal source of water and the largest element of depletion (Konikow and Neuzil, 2007).

5. **Water budget**: Use pumpage data in conjunction with a water budget analysis for an aquifer system to estimate depletion (for example, Kjelstrom, 1995). This approach is limited to systems for which there are reasonable estimates of other fluxes in and out of the system; the approach is applied most often in arid to semiarid areas where natural recharge is small or negligible.

6. **Pumpage fraction**: Use pumpage data in conjunction with an assumption that the fraction of pumpage derived from storage can be correlated with the fraction during a control period or for a control area (for example, Anderson and others, 1992).

7. **Extrapolation**: In cases where data do not extend through 2008, extrapolate rates of depletion through the end of the study period using the observed rates calculated for the most recent multi-year period. Adjust rates for extrapolation accordingly if recent observed water-level changes do not support a linear extrapolation. In cases where sufficient data exist, the annual rate of depletion is estimated through correlation with the observed rates of water-level change and (or) annual rates of pumpage.

8. **Subsidence**: Calculate a volume of subsidence in areas where land subsidence is caused by groundwater withdrawals; the depletion volume must equal or exceed the subsidence volume, so this serves as a cross-check and constraint on calculated depletion volumes (Kasmarek and Strom, 2002; Kasmarek and Robinson, 2004).

The first three methods above (water-level change, gravity, and modeling) are the most reliable, and estimated storage changes are probably accurate to within ±20 percent in most cases. Famiglietti and others (2011) reported that the estimated changes in groundwater storage using GRACE satellite data for a 7-year period were within ±19 percent of the estimated value. The water balance computed by a well-calibrated simulation model typically has an error of less than 0.1 percent. However, this reflects numerical accuracy and precision, and not the overall reliability of the model or accuracy of computed water budget elements, which are more difficult to assess (Hill and Tiedeman, 2007). The confining unit and water budget methods are less reliable, but probably yield values within ±30 percent (see Kjelstrom, 1995; Konikow and Neuzil, 2007). The pumping fraction method is a coarser estimation method, based on assumed correlations with withdrawals that are only reliable to ±25 percent; because of additional uncertainty in related factors, this estimate is probably only reliable within ±40 percent. The accuracy of the extrapolation method decreases with extrapolation time, but in most cases is probably accurate to within ±30 percent. The subsidence method can estimate subsidence volume within ±20 percent or less, but is only used to provide a minimum bound on the estimate of total groundwater depletion.

Where possible, cross-checks were done between alternative approaches. For example, in the large depletion area of the Central Valley, California, the time period for depletion estimates made using a calibrated transient model (Faunt and others, 2009b) overlapped with the GRACE gravity-based estimates (Famiglietti and others, 2011) for a few years; the values computed using the two methods varied from their mean value by only ±16 percent. In the Gulf Coastal Plain near Houston, Texas, the volume of land subsidence was estimated using geographic information system (GIS) tools to analyze a map of historical subsidence (1906–2000) available from the Harris-Galveston Subsidence District (*http://www.hgsubsidence.org/about/subsidence/land-surface-subsidence.html*). The calculated cumulative subsidence volume was 10.5 km³. The cumulative water budget from a simulation model calibrated for 1891–2000 indicates that a total volume of 10.8 km³ of groundwater was removed from storage in the unconsolidated clay units as the clays compacted and subsidence progressed—essentially all of it during the 20th century (Kasmarek and Robinson, 2004). The difference of less than 3 percent provides good support for the quality of the model calibration and its reliability.

Relevant data to apply these methods are widely available in the United States. In this analysis, comprehensive assessments of groundwater depletion during the 20th century were completed for most of the highly developed aquifer systems in the United States, and descriptions of 41 separate aquifer systems, subareas, and categories are described below. In addition, several large aquifer systems were assessed and found to have negligible long-term volumetric depletion, even though there may have been other signs of overdevelopment (for example, the Edwards-Trinity aquifer system in Texas and the Floridan aquifer system in central and southern Florida). In other areas (for example, the Roswell Basin, New Mexico), groundwater depletion is known to exist, but sufficient data to provide a reasonably accurate estimate of the magnitude and temporal history of the depletion are not readily available.

In coastal aquifers, fresh groundwater typically occurs in a wedge or lens overlying salty groundwater. Groundwater withdrawals in such areas usually cause both a decline in the water table and a rise in the position of the underlying interface between fresh and salty groundwater. Both contribute to a depletion of fresh groundwater. As an interface rises, the freshwater is replaced with saltwater, and the net volumetric change of water in storage associated with a rising base of a freshwater lens is negligible. Because the goal of this assessment was to assess changes in the total volume of groundwater in storage—not just in the volume of usable fresh groundwater—storage changes related to the position of a subsurface freshwater-saltwater interface are not evaluated.

Because of a paucity of data, assessments were not made of increased groundwater storage due to seepage losses from reservoirs, decreased storage caused by mineral extraction activities (such as dewatering, but which eventually is mostly recoverable), or depletion from numerous low-capacity domestic wells outside of the explicitly assessed areas. In areas explicitly evaluated, these factors would inherently be counted. These factors should be evaluated more carefully in the future.

Individual Depletion Estimates

This section provides background information and additional details on the methods and calculations used to estimate long-term groundwater depletion in the individual aquifer systems and areas that were integrated into the overall estimate. For each system or area, the 20th century depletion (1900–2000), the additional depletion through 2008, and the annual rate of depletion from 1900 through 2008 were estimated. The depletion volumes for all analyzed systems

Table 1.   Groundwater depletion in individual aquifer systems, subareas, or by land use category, United States (1900–2008).

[Values may not sum to totals because of independent rounding; category is "Agricultural and Land Drainage"; km³, cubic kilometer]

	Index number (see fig. 1)	Primary methods[a]	Total net volumetric groundwater depletion[b] (km³)	
			1900–2000	1900–2008
Atlantic Coastal Plain:				
Georgia and northeast Florida	1	3,1	3.5	3.5
Long Island, New York	2	3,1	1.6	1.1
Maryland and Delaware	3	3,5,4,7	1.6	1.9
New Jersey	4	3,4,7	1.2	1.2
North Carolina	5	3,7	1.2	1.6
South Carolina	6	3,7	2.8	3.2
Virginia	7	3	2.5	4.5
TOTAL Atlantic Coastal Plain			14.4	17.2
Gulf Coastal Plain:				
Coastal lowlands of Alabama, Florida, Louisiana, and Mississippi	8	3,4,7	37.8	38.5
Houston area and northern part of Texas Gulf Coast	9	3,7,8	28.9	31.1
Central part of Gulf Coast aquifer system in Texas	10	3,7	4.8	4.8
Winter Garden area, southern part of Texas Gulf Coast	11	3,4,7	9.5	9.6
Mississippi embayment	12	3	117.6	182.0
TOTAL Gulf Coastal Plain			198.6	266.0
High Plains (Ogallala) Aquifer	13			
Colorado		1	14.3	23.9
Kansas		1	60.5	79.8
Nebraska		1	-1.1	20.4
New Mexico		1	10.8	14.5
Oklahoma		1	13.9	16.0
South Dakota		1	0.1	0.6
Texas		1	160.3	181.9

Table 1. Groundwater depletion in individual aquifer systems, subareas, or by land use category, United States (1900–2008).—Continued

[Values may not sum to totals because of independent rounding; category is "Agricultural and Land Drainage"; km³, cubic kilometer]

	Index number (see fig. 1)	Primary methods[a]	Total net volumetric groundwater depletion[b] (km³)	
			1900–2000	1900–2008
Wyoming		1	0.1	3.2
TOTAL High Plains Aquifer	13	1	259.1	340.9
Central Valley, California	14	3,2	113.4	144.8
Western Alluvial Basins:				
Alluvial basins, Arizona	15	3,6	105.3	102.0
Antelope Valley, California	16	3,7	10.5	10.6
Coachella Valley, California	17	3,6,7	3.2	3.7
Death Valley region, California and Nevada	18	3,7	3.4	4.0
Escalante Valley, Utah	19	1,3,6	3.2	3.7
Estancia Basin, New Mexico	20	3,6,5	1.7	1.9
Hueco Bolson, New Mexico and Texas	21	3,7	4.6	5.7
Las Vegas Valley, Nevada	22	1,5,7	2.3	2.1
Los Angeles Basin, California	23	6,1	4.1	4.2
Mesilla Basin, New Mexico	24	3,7	0.3	0.4
Middle Rio Grande Basin, New Mexico	25	3,7	2.4	2.7
Milford area, Utah	26	3,7	1.0	1.2
Mimbres Basin, New Mexico	27	3,7	4.2	4.2
Mojave River Basin, California	28	3,7	3.2	3.6
Pahvant Valley, Utah	29	3,7	0.8	1.1
Paradise Valley, Nevada	30	3,7	0.2	0.3
Pecos River Basin, Texas	31	5,1,7	20.2	21.0
San Luis Valley, Colorado	32	3,7	3.3	3.6
Tularosa Basin, New Mexico	33	3,7	1.1	1.5
TOTAL Western Alluvial Basins			175.1	177.5
Western Volcanic Aquifer Systems:				
Columbia Plateau aquifer system	34	3,7	-5.2	-3.8
Oahu, Hawaii	35	3,1,6	0.2	0.2
Snake River Plain, Idaho	36	3,5,7	-41.4	-39.9
TOTAL Western Volcanic Systems			-46.3	-43.5
Deep Confined Bedrock Aquifers:				
Black Mesa area, Arizona	37	3,7	0.2	0.3
Midwest Cambrian-Ordovician aquifer system	38	3,4,7	11.4	12.6
Dakota aquifer, northern Great Plains	39	4,3,6,7	19.6	20.3
Denver Basin, Colorado	40	3,7	0.8	1.3
TOTAL Deep Confined Aquifers			31.9	34.4
Agricultural and Land Drainage		1	55.0	55.0
TOTAL (all systems)			801.2	992.2

[a] Codes for methods correspond to ordered listing in Methods discussion (1 = water-level change and storativity; 2 = gravity; 3 = flow model; 4 = confining unit; 5 = water budget; 6 = pumpage fraction; 7 = extrapolation; 8 = subsidence). Where multiple methods are listed, order reflects relative importance for the particular case.

[b] Negative values indicate an increase in the volume of groundwater in storage.

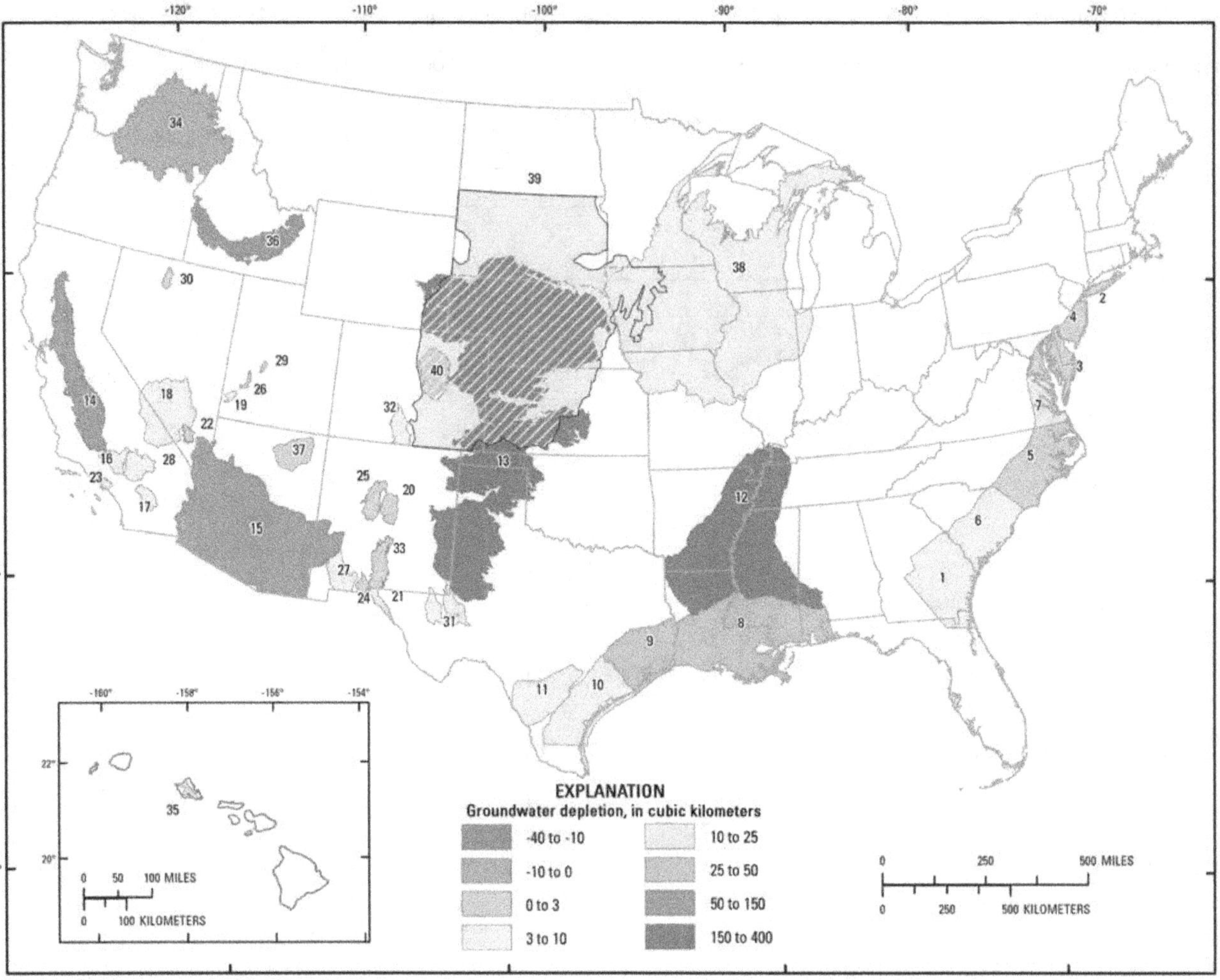

Base from U.S. Geological Survey digital data, 1972,1:2,000,000
Albers Equal-Area Conic Projection
Standard parallels 29° 30′ N and 45° 30′ N, central meridian 96° 00′ W

Figure 2. Map of the United States (excluding Alaska) showing cumulative groundwater depletion, 1900 through 2008, in 40 assessed aquifer systems or subareas. Index numbers are defined in table 1. Colors are hatched in the Dakota aquifer (area 39) where the aquifer overlaps with other aquifers having different values of depletion.

and areas are summarized in table 1, which also indicates the primary methods used to estimate depletion in each area. The spatial distribution of the magnitude of depletion during 1900–2008 is shown in figure 2. For all cases, the cumulative annual depletion was estimated for each of the 108 years of the study period. These annual values provided the basis for estimating average rates of depletion for selected time periods (table 2).

Atlantic Coastal Plain

Georgia and Northeast Florida

The 24-county Atlantic Coastal Plain region in Georgia covers an area of about 52,000 km^2 and encompasses an additional 26,000 km^2 offshore on the Continental Shelf (Krause and Randolph, 1989) (figs. 1 and 2). An adjacent 5,000 km^2 area in northeast Florida is considered contiguous with the coastal plain aquifer system of Georgia for the groundwater flow analysis by Payne and others (2005), so is similarly considered jointly here. The average annual precipitation on the coastal plain region in Georgia and northeast Florida ranges from about 112 cm/yr in the northern part to about 137 cm/yr in the southern part. The hydrologic setting of the coastal plain region in Georgia is described in more detail by Krause and Randolph (1989) and Payne and others (2005).

The coastal plain system consists of interbedded clastics and marl in the updip portion and massive limestone and dolomite in the downdip portion (Krause and Randolph, 1989). The coastal plain of Georgia is divided into three aquifer systems: the surficial aquifer, the Brunswick aquifer system (consisting of upper and lower units), and the Floridan aquifer system (consisting of upper and lower units). Most of the groundwater withdrawn in the coastal region of Georgia is

Table 2. Estimated average volumetric rates of groundwater depletion in the United States for selected time periods.

[Values may not sum to totals because of independent rounding; km³/yr, cubic kilometer per year; I.D., insufficient data for reliable calculation]

	Average volumetric rate of groundwater depletion (km³/yr)								
	1900–2000	1900–2008	1900–1950	1951–1960	1961–1970	1971–1980	1981–1990	1991–2000	2001–2008
Atlantic Coastal Plain:									
Georgia and northeast Florida	0.035	0.033	0.029	0.039	0.062	0.045	0.060	0.000	0.000
Long Island, New York	0.016	0.011	0.012	0.031	0.040	0.012	0.007	0.007	-0.053
Maryland and Delaware	0.016	0.018	0.005	0.015	0.019	0.027	0.034	0.041	0.042
New Jersey	0.012	0.011	0.006	0.022	0.037	0.034	0.017	-0.017	0.000
North Carolina	0.012	0.015	0.005	0.033	-0.016	0.016	0.031	0.032	0.053
South Carolina	0.028	0.030	0.013	0.062	-0.003	0.029	0.101	0.020	0.062
Virginia	0.025	0.042	0.008	0.061	0.144	-0.027	0.083	-0.045	0.244
TOTAL Atlantic Coastal Plain	0.144	0.159	0.078	0.261	0.282	0.136	0.333	0.038	0.349
Gulf Coastal Plain:									
Coastal lowlands of Alabama, Florida, Louisiana, and Mississippi	0.378	0.356	0.426	0.298	0.788	0.563	-0.093	0.090	0.090
Houston area and northern part of Texas Gulf Coast	0.289	0.288	0.079	0.361	0.502	0.740	0.544	0.344	0.280
Central part of Gulf Coast aquifer system in Texas	0.048	0.044	0.016	0.183	0.183	0.183	-0.036	-0.113	0.000
Winter Garden area, southern part of Texas Gulf Coast	0.095	0.089	0.031	0.445	0.283	0.024	0.024	0.024	0.012
Mississippi embayment	1.176	1.685	0.068	-0.044	-0.179	1.383	4.399	5.858	8.048
TOTAL Gulf Coastal Plain	1.985	2.463	0.620	1.242	1.577	2.894	4.838	6.202	8.430
High Plains (Ogallala) Aquifer									
Colorado	0.143	0.222	I.D.	I.D.	I.D.	I.D.	I.D.	I.D.	1.203
Kansas	0.606	0.739	I.D.	I.D.	I.D.	I.D.	I.D.	I.D.	2.406
Nebraska	-0.011	0.190	I.D.	I.D.	I.D.	I.D.	I.D.	I.D.	2.699
New Mexico	0.107	0.134	I.D.	I.D.	I.D.	I.D.	I.D.	I.D.	0.463
Oklahoma	0.139	0.149	I.D.	I.D.	I.D.	I.D.	I.D.	I.D.	0.262
South Dakota	0.001	0.006	I.D.	I.D.	I.D.	I.D.	I.D.	I.D.	0.062
Texas	1.603	1.684	I.D.	I.D.	I.D.	I.D.	I.D.	I.D.	2.699
Wyoming	0.001	0.030	I.D.	I.D.	I.D.	I.D.	I.D.	I.D.	0.386
TOTAL High Plains Aquifer	2.591	3.156	0.202	6.109	6.192	5.570	2.897	4.136	10.220
Central Valley, California	1.134	1.340	0.522	2.900	0.998	2.361	2.870	-0.398	3.919
Western Alluvial Basins:									
Alluvial Basins, Arizona	1.053	0.945	0.516	2.750	3.076	2.946	-0.410	-0.410	-0.410
Antelope Valley, California	0.105	0.098	0.082	0.285	0.240	0.095	0.011	0.011	0.005
Coachella Valley, California	0.032	0.034	0.003	0.032	0.055	0.071	0.083	0.060	0.060
Death Valley region, California-Nevada	0.034	0.037	0.005	0.030	0.060	0.063	0.075	0.082	0.080
Escalante Valley, Utah	0.032	0.034	0.003	0.044	0.057	0.066	0.072	0.066	0.062
Estancia Basin, New Mexico	0.017	0.018	0.000	0.029	0.027	0.036	0.045	0.031	0.028
Hueco Bolson, New Mexico and Texas	0.046	0.053	0.002	0.033	0.056	0.103	0.129	0.130	0.135
Las Vegas Valley, Nevada	0.023	0.019	0.012	0.043	0.043	0.053	0.054	-0.026	-0.026
Los Angeles Basin, California	0.041	0.039	0.053	0.172	-0.016	-0.001	-0.010	0.000	0.014
Mesilla Basin, New Mexico	0.003	0.004	0.000	0.006	0.007	0.009	0.005	0.003	0.010

Table 2. Estimated average volumetric rates of groundwater depletion in the United States for selected time periods.—Continued

[Values may not sum to totals because of independent rounding; km³/yr, cubic kilometer per year; I.D., insufficient data for reliable calculation]

	Average volumetric rate of groundwater depletion (km³/yr)								
	1900–2000	1900–2008	1900–1950	1951–1960	1961–1970	1971–1980	1981–1990	1991–2000	2001–2008
Middle Rio Grande Basin, New Mexico	0.024	0.025	-0.002	0.009	0.040	0.058	0.058	0.086	0.042
Milford area, Utah	0.010	0.011	0.000	0.020	0.020	0.023	0.019	0.021	0.021
Mimbres Basin, New Mexico	0.042	0.039	0.009	0.063	0.079	0.106	0.067	0.060	0.000
Mojave River Basin, California	0.032	0.033	-0.005	0.089	0.059	0.042	0.132	0.027	0.041
Pahvant Valley, Utah	0.008	0.010	0.001	0.040	0.030	0.044	-0.075	0.037	0.037
Paradise Valley, Nevada	0.002	0.003	0.000	0.000	-0.005	0.014	0.009	0.005	0.005
Pecos River Basin, Texas	0.202	0.194	0.010	0.693	0.699	0.373	0.106	0.101	0.093
San Luis Valley, Colorado	0.033	0.034	0.001	0.045	0.054	0.135	0.045	0.045	0.045
Tularosa Basin, New Mexico	0.011	0.014	0.001	0.023	0.015	0.011	0.011	0.043	0.050
TOTAL Western Alluvial Basins	1.751	1.643	0.692	4.408	4.598	4.248	0.427	0.373	0.292
Western Volcanic Aquifer Systems:									
Columbia Plateau aquifer system	-0.052	-0.035	-0.013	-0.631	-0.316	0.153	0.170	0.170	0.170
Oahu, Hawaii	0.002	0.002	0.003	0.003	0.001	0.001	0.001	0.001	-0.003
Snake River Plain, Idaho	-0.414	-0.370	-0.878	-0.311	-0.027	0.234	0.180	0.180	0.180
TOTAL Western Volcanic Systems	-0.463	-0.403	-0.888	-0.940	-0.342	0.388	0.351	0.351	0.347
Deep Confined Bedrock Aquifers:									
Black Mesa area, Arizona	0.002	0.002	0.000	0.000	0.001	0.005	0.007	0.008	0.008
Midwest Cambrian-Ordovician aquifer system	0.114	0.117	0.087	0.120	0.247	0.318	0.000	0.016	0.156
Dakota Aquifer, northern Great Plains	0.196	0.188	0.271	0.141	0.139	0.136	0.097	0.089	0.089
Denver Basin, Colorado	0.008	0.008	0.002	-0.009	0.024	0.039	0.010	0.009	0.007
TOTAL Deep Confined Aquifers	0.319	0.319	0.359	0.252	0.411	0.498	0.113	0.121	0.312
Agricultural and Land Drainage	0.550	0.509	0.839	0.429	0.391	0.361	0.113	0.010	0.000
TOTAL (all systems)	8.01	9.19	2.42	14.7	14.1	16.5	11.9	10.8	23.9

from the Upper Floridan aquifer due to its relatively shallow depths, large areal extent, and good water quality (Clarke and Krause, 2000). A more detailed description of the geologic and hydrogeologic features in the study area is provided by Krause and Randolph (1989).

Many wells in the downgradient part of the aquifer system have been set in large-scale cavernous zones, solution channels, and other cavities (Krause and Randolph, 1989). Withdrawals from the coastal plain aquifer system have increased since the 1880s; heavy withdrawals have led to declines in water levels (some as much as 52 m), saltwater intrusion, and land subsidence (Krause and Randolph, 1989). Groundwater pumpage from the Upper Floridan aquifer in 1980 in Georgia and adjacent parts of southeastern South Carolina and northeast Florida reached about 0.86 km³/yr (Krause and Randolph, 1989), although Fanning (1999) shows that the groundwater withdrawals within the 24-county area in Georgia was slightly less than 0.55 km³/yr in 1980. Within the 24-county coastal plain of Georgia, groundwater withdraw-

als declined slightly to about 0.51 km³/yr in 1990, and further decreased to about 0.48 km³/yr in 1997 (Fanning, 1999; Peck and others, 1999). As pumping rates decreased throughout the 1990s, water levels in the aquifer system began to recover. Water-level rises in the Upper Floridan aquifer (as measured in 248 wells) ranged from minimal to 3.7 m from May 1990 to May 1998 (Peck and others, 1999). A long-term well hydrograph in the Brunswick area (Well 311319081232901; *http://groundwaterwatch.usgs.gov/AWLSites.asp?S=3113190 81232901&ncd=ltn&a=1&d=1*) shows little to no net change from about 1980 through 2004.

Payne (2010) presents a time series of groundwater pumpage in a five-county area around Savannah—one of the major pumping centers. Payne reports that around the year 1900, about 0.0083 km³/yr were withdrawn in the Savannah area. Payne (2010, fig. 6) further shows the estimated pumpage for 1915–2004, noting that pumpage stabilized at about 0.14 km³/yr since 2000.

A groundwater-flow model of the coastal plain region of Georgia and adjacent parts of South Carolina and northeast Florida was developed by Payne and others (2005) using the three-dimensional (3D), finite-difference groundwater-flow model, MODFLOW-2000 (Harbaugh and others, 2000). The area of active cells in the model covers a total area of about 109,000 km[2], including both onshore and offshore portions of subsurface units. An initial steady-state simulation was run to simulate predevelopment conditions (circa 1900), and a final steady-state simulation was calibrated for conditions in the year 2000.

The model includes seven layers, representing four aquifers and three intervening confining units, and each layer is discretized into a grid of 119 rows and 108 columns for a total of 12,852 cells per layer. Cell sizes range from about 1,220 m × 1,520 m to 5,030 m × 5,030 m, with finer discretization located near observed cones of depression at Savannah and Brunswick, Georgia. Boundary conditions applied to the model include a general-head boundary on the top active cells because the focus of this model study was on the deeper confined Floridan aquifer system. However, this precludes consideration of temporal changes in water-table elevations.

GIS tools were used to construct maps showing the difference in head between predevelopment (assumed to be representative of 1900) and 2000 for each of the seven model layers. Estimates of the volume of water removed from storage from 1900 through 2000 were calculated on the basis of the changes in calibrated heads from 1900 to 2000, the cell dimensions, and estimates of storage properties for each layer.

The median value of the storage coefficient (S) for aquifers in the study area is 0.0004 (Payne and others, 2005, p. 81). This value of S was used to estimate storage depletion in the Brunswick aquifer and in the Upper and Lower Floridan aquifers, and some higher values were also evaluated for unconfined parts of the system. Data on the specific storage (S_S) of the confining units are not readily available, so our calculations examined a reasonable range of values (1.6×10^{-5} m^{-1} to 3.3×10^{-5} m^{-1}). The simulated total volume of water removed from storage from the seven units between 1900 and 2000 under six possible combinations of assumptions about storage properties range from 3.1 to 6.8 km[3]. Therefore, the total 20th century groundwater depletion in this study area is considered to be 5.1 km[3] ±2.0 km[3].

The time series of pumpage for a five-county area (Payne, 2010) is used as a surrogate for trends in depletion in the larger study area. That is, the growth in depletion during 1900–2000 is assumed to parallel the nondimensional growth in pumpage in the five-county area. However, because pumping rates decreased noticeably during the 1990s, it is further assumed that no additional net depletion occurred after 1990 so that the estimate of 5.1 km[3] applies to 1990, 2000, and 2008. The results show the most rapid growth in depletion volume occurred between 1930 and 1975 (fig. 3).

The northern part of the Georgia coastal plain is also included in the area simulated in other regional transient models (Petkewich and Campbell, 2007; Coes and others,

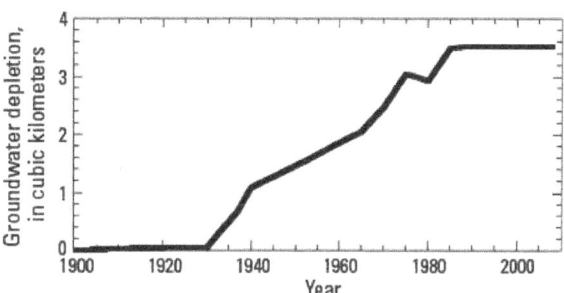

Figure 3. Cumulative groundwater depletion in the coastal plain aquifer system of Georgia and adjacent northeast Florida, 1900 through 2008.

2010). To avoid counting the depletion in this area twice, only the depletion volume in northeast Florida and parts of Georgia not included in the other models is estimated and attributed to this area. It is assumed that depletion is proportional to withdrawals and, based on withdrawal records, an average of 69.1 percent of the total computed depletion is included for purposes of estimating the total depletion in the United States. After this adjustment, the 20th century depletion in Georgia and northeast Florida is about 3.5 km[3] (table 1). The reconstructed time history of depletion is shown in figure 3.

Long Island, New York

Long Island, New York, has a total area of about 3,600 km[2] and extends 190 km east-northeast from the southeast corner of New York State (Scorca and Monti, 2001) (figs. 1 and 2). The mean annual precipitation between 1951 and 1965 was approximately 109 cm. Groundwater is a primary source of water supply on much of the island.

Three principal aquifers underlie Long Island; in descending order these are the upper glacial aquifer, the Magothy, and the Lloyd. A fourth aquifer, the Jameco, is present only in Kings and southern Queens counties at the western end of the island. The Magothy and Jameco aquifers are separated from the upper glacial aquifer, where present, by the Gardiners Clay. The clay unit is thickest (around 30 m) in Queens County and thins to about 15 m over the remainder of its extent. Pleistocene glacial deposits of clay, silt, sand, gravel, cobbles, and boulders blanket much of Long Island. The glacial deposits range in thickness from a featheredge to about 180 m in the center of the island (Olcott, 1995). The hydrology and geology are discussed in more detail by Franke and McClymonds (1972) and Olcott (1995).

Groundwater has been a major source of the water supply for Long Island since the mid-19th century. Rapid increases in population and development led to increased withdrawals and subsequent declines in water levels. In 1917, the first water tunnel was completed that transported water from upstate New York to New York City, including parts of Kings and Queens Counties on Long Island. There was a minor reduction in pumpage, but demand continued to grow (Buxton and

Shernoff, 1999). Groundwater pumping for public supply ceased in Kings County in 1947 and in Queens County in 1974. These areas now are supplied water from mainland surface-water reservoirs and wells established farther to the east. After cessation of pumping in 1947, water levels in Kings County began to recover. In 1961, a sizeable cone of depression still remained in Queens County. The cone migrated eastward with the cessation of pumpage in Queens County in 1974 (Buxton and Shernoff, 1999).

Heavy pumpage and loss of recharge to principal aquifers, predominantly in Kings, Queens, and much of Nassau County in western Long Island, led to severe declines in the water table by 1936 (Buxton and Shernoff, 1999). Buxton and Smolensky (1999, fig. 18) show the annual average public-supply pumpage during 1904–83, indicating especially steep increases during 1945–65. During the 1980s and 1990s, pumpage decreased in the western part of the island but continued to increase in Nassau and Suffolk Counties in the central and eastern parts of the island (Busciolano, 2005). Approximately 0.65 km³/yr of fresh groundwater was withdrawn from the aquifers on Long Island during 1985 (Olcott, 1995). Busciolano (2005, table 2) indicates that total withdrawals on Long Island during 1995–99 were about 0.5 km³/yr.

Continuous eastward development on Long Island throughout the 20th century has resulted in a decrease in the base flow of streams and substantially lowered groundwater levels (Scorca and Monti, 2001). In Nassau County, an extensive operation of sanitary sewers began in the 1950s and reached its maximum discharge by the mid-1960s. Prior to installation of the sewer system, the unconfined upper glacial aquifer received a significant amount of recharge from septic tanks. After installation of the sewer system, wastewater was discharged to the ocean, leading to a reduction in recharge and long-term water-level declines from about 1955 through 1975 that averaged about 4.3 m (Alley and others, 1999, fig. 18).

A quasi-3D groundwater-flow model was created for Long Island aquifers (Buxton and Smolensky, 1999) using MODFLOW (McDonald and Harbaugh, 1988). Steady-state models were made for pre-1900 conditions and for 1968 to 1983 conditions. The model contains four layers to represent the different aquifers; grid cells were 1,200 m on a side. Confining units were not explicitly represented in the model as separate layers. Another groundwater-flow model using MODFLOW was created for Kings and Queens Counties (Misut and Monti, 1999). That model was later revised and updated through 1997 by Cartwright (2002). During 1992–97, the groundwater system in the western part of Long Island was relatively static in relation to conditions earlier in the 20th century (Cartwright, 2002).

Groundwater depletion for the Long Island aquifer system was evaluated using model-generated potentiometric data. Model-calibrated maps representing predevelopment and 1983 potentiometric surfaces in Nassau and Suffolk Counties (Buxton and Smolensky, 1999, figs. 16 and 20) and maps of the 1903 and 1997 potentiometric surfaces of the upper glacial

aquifer in Kings and Queens Counties (Cartwright, 2002, figs. 3a and 3i) were differenced to estimate long-term water-level changes.

A volume of groundwater depletion for each aquifer on the island was then estimated on the basis of the head difference, surface area, and specific yield (for unconfined aquifers) or storage coefficient (for confined aquifers). Specific yield values for the upper glacial aquifer ranged from 0.18 to 0.30 (Buxton and Smolensky, 1999); a middle value of 0.25 was applied. For the Magothy aquifer, a specific yield value of 0.10 was assumed for the unconfined parts, and a storage coefficient of 6×10^{-4} (dimensionless) was assigned for the confined parts; the Lloyd aquifer was assigned a storage coefficient value of 3×10^{-4} (dimensionless). The declines in water-levels indicated a total depletion in storage in aquifers of 1.3 km³ from the turn of the century until 1983 in Nassau and Suffolk Counties and through 1997 in Kings and Queens Counties. Storage losses from the confined parts of the Magothy and Lloyd aquifers were relatively small and not included in the final total.

The method of Konikow and Neuzil (2007) was used to estimate the volume of water depleted from confining layers as a function of head decline in adjacent aquifer(s), hydrologic properties of the confining units, and the duration of the drawdown. Based on literature values, a specific storage value of 5×10^{-5} m⁻¹ was assumed for the confining layers. The total volume of water removed from storage from confining units was thereby calculated to be about 0.2 km³. Thus, the total groundwater depletion volume is estimated to be about 1.5 km³ for the Long Island coastal plain aquifer system from predevelopment to the 1990s.

In reconstructing the time rate of depletion (fig. 4), the total depletion is assumed to have grown at a rate parallel to that of the total withdrawals (Buxton and Smolensky, 1999, fig. 18), further assuming that from 1983 through 1999, rates changed in accordance with the newer data (Busciolano, 2005), and that from 1999 through 2005 there was no change. Because above normal precipitation from late 2005 through 2008 caused large rises in groundwater levels (Monti and others, 2008), it is assumed that water in storage increased substantially during the last 3 years of this assessment period

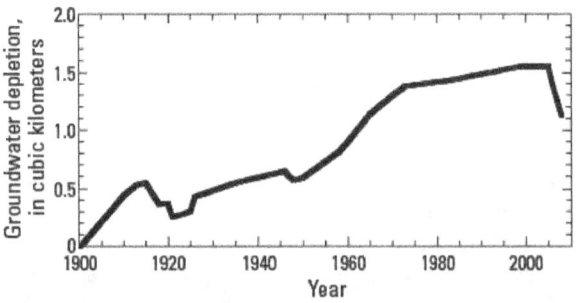

Figure 4. Cumulative groundwater depletion in the coastal plain aquifer system of Long Island, New York, 1900 through 2008.

and depletion decreased by 10 percent per year. Under these assumptions, depletion is about 1.6 km³ in 2000 and 1.1 km³ in 2008 (table 1).

Maryland and Delaware

The Atlantic Coastal Plain aquifer system includes an area of approximately 22,000 km² in Maryland, Delaware, and the District of Columbia (figs. 1 and 2). The area includes two major estuaries—Delaware Bay and Chesapeake Bay. The average annual rate of precipitation, measured between 1951 and 1980, is about 112 cm east of Chesapeake Bay and 106 cm west of Chesapeake Bay (Fleck and Vroblesky, 1996). The aquifer system consists of a thick sequence of sand, gravel, silt, and clay that generally thickens seaward to as much as 2,600 m along the Atlantic coast in Maryland (Fleck and Vroblesky, 1996). Use of groundwater resources in the study area has resulted in large water-level declines.

Groundwater withdrawals from the coastal plain aquifer system in Maryland increased from about 0.035 km³/yr in 1900 to 0.19 km³/yr in 1980 (Wheeler and Wilde, 1989). Groundwater pumpage increased 60 percent between 1970 and 1980 (Fleck and Vroblesky, 1996) and by about 32 percent during 1980–2000 (Soeder and others, 2007). Groundwater withdrawals reached approximately 0.34 km³/yr by 1995 (Wheeler, 1998). In 1995, groundwater withdrawals in Delaware were about 0.15 km³/yr (Wheeler, 1999). Fleck and Vroblesky (1996) present annual withdrawals during 1900–80. In total, about 6.2 km³ of groundwater was pumped from the coastal plain aquifers from 1900 until 1980 (Fleck and Vroblesky, 1996, tables 2 and 3). Several large regional cones of depression have developed as a result of lowered water levels from the pumpage.

Soeder and others (2007) analyzed groundwater withdrawals and changes in groundwater levels during 1980–2005. They showed that total annual groundwater withdrawals generally increased during this more recent 25-year study period. Soeder and others (2007, p. 3) report that "the general trend for confined aquifer wells is a steady decline in water levels through the mid-1980s, accelerating in the late 1980s." Soeder

and others (2007) also show a number of representative well hydrographs that show generally linear trends of water-level declines during 1980–2004 (for example, fig. 5). They further report that cones of depression in the confined aquifers have developed or expanded because of the additional and increased pumpage since 1980.

The groundwater flow system in the coastal plain of Maryland and Delaware was simulated by Fleck and Vroblesky (1996) using the quasi-three-dimensional, finite-difference program of Trescott (1975). An initial 10-layer model, representing 10 unconfined and confined aquifers and associated confining units, was calibrated to represent steady-state (predevelopment) conditions prior to 1900 and was converted to an 11-layer transient model to simulate 1900–80. The 10 aquifers were represented as 10 layers in the model; the confining units were not explicitly modeled. Each layer was discretized into a grid consisting of 42 rows and 36 columns for a total of 1,512 cells per layer (1,038 of which are active). All cells measure 5.6 km on a side and represent an area of 31.7 km². Other assumptions, hydraulic properties, boundary conditions, and calibration methods are described in more detail by Fleck and Vroblesky (1996).

The model results indicate that the net rate of depletion of groundwater storage in the confined aquifers during 1978–80 was about 0.50 m³/s. This is equivalent to about 8.6 percent of the total pumpage simulated in the model for this time period (noting that the simulated pumpage is reported to represent only about 60 percent of the actual total pumpage). Under simplifying assumptions that a direct linear relation exists between pumpage and the change in storage, and that the calculated ratio of storage change to pumpage from model stress period 10 (1978–80) applies to stress periods 1 through 9, it is estimated that a total of about 0.5 km³ was removed from storage in aquifers during 1900–80.

An alternative approach to estimating long-term depletion is based on changes in head from predevelopment through 1980, as indicated by maps and hydrographs in Fleck and Vroblesky (1996). The volumetric change in storage in each aquifer in which there was substantial pumpage and drawdown can be estimated as the product of its area, average change in

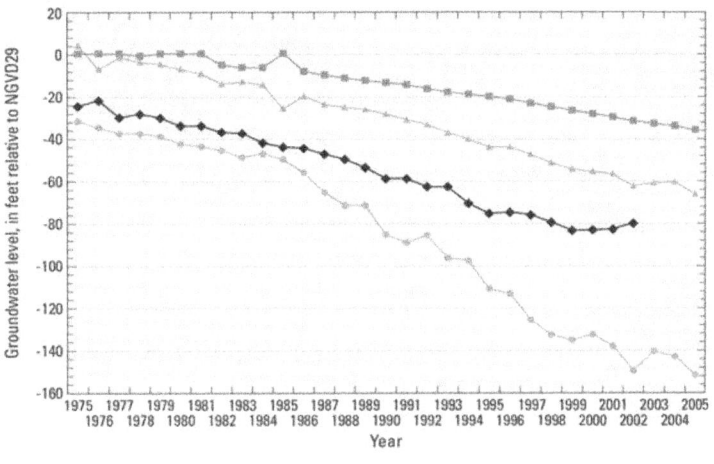

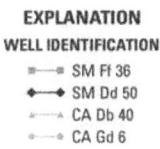

EXPLANATION

WELL IDENTIFICATION

- SM Ff 36
- SM Dd 50
- CA Db 40
- CA Gd 6

Figure 5. Nearly linear declines in the potentiometric surfaces over 30 years in four representative wells from Calvert and St. Mary's Counties, Maryland (from Soeder and others, 2007).

head, and average storage coefficient. This analysis indicates that approximately 0.5 km³ of groundwater was depleted from storage in the confined aquifers of the Maryland-Delaware coastal plain, which matches that derived above on the basis of extrapolation of the 1978–80 model-computed rates of depletion to the entire period from 1900 to 1980.

Because of the increased withdrawals and generally linear increase in drawdown observed during 1980–2000, the total cumulative depletion during the 20th century is estimated by extrapolating the 0.5 m³/s rate of depletion for 1978–80 to the 1980–2000 time period—an additional 20 years. This extrapolation would indicate that an additional 0.3 km³ of water was removed from storage in the coastal plain aquifer system during the final 20 years of the 20th century—for a total of 0.8 km³. This represents about 10 percent of the estimated total withdrawals from the aquifers.

Transient propagation of drawdown through low-permeability confining units also must be accompanied by some removal of water from storage within the confining layers, and that drainage might represent a relatively large source of water for the wells pumping the confined aquifers. In fact, Soeder and others (2007) state that there is evidence that deep drawdowns in some pumped aquifers may be causing declines in adjacent, unpumped aquifers—a condition that implies drawdown in and drainage of intervening confining layers. But confining layers were not explicitly represented in the model of Fleck and Vroblesky (1996).

The volume of water depleted from confining layers was estimated using the method of Konikow and Neuzil (2007). Hydraulic data available on the confining units are limited. Hansen (1977) reports a number of specific storage (S_S) values from consolidation tests on cores obtained from confining layers at sites in Maryland. At effective stresses of interest here, Hansen's (1977) data show S_S values of $1.2–3.0 \times 10^{-4}$ m^{-1} for the Marlboro Clay and $1.5–2.5 \times 10^{-4}$ m^{-1} in the Brightseat–Upper Potomac confining unit. Pope and Burbey (2004) estimated specific storage values for skeletal compressibility in equivalent confining layers in the nearby Virginia coastal plain from compaction data as great as $S_S = 1.0 \times 10^{-4}$ m^{-1} for the shallower confining units and as great as 1.5×10^{-5} m^{-1} for the deeper confining units. On the basis of this prior information, it is conservatively assumed that $S_S = 1.0 \times 10^{-5}$ m^{-1}, recognizing that this value could lie within a range of uncertainty of as much as an order of magnitude. The assumed value lies in the range reported in the literature for normally consolidated sediments at a porosity of 0.30. The calculated total volume of water removed from storage from the six confining units during the 20th century is thereby estimated to be 0.8 km³.

The total 20th century depletion in the Maryland-Delaware coastal plain aquifer system is on the order of 1.6 km³ (0.8 km³ for the aquifers plus 0.8 km³ for the confining units). The time rate of depletion since 1900 was estimated by assuming a correlation with the pumpage history extrapolated through 2008. This indicates that the cumulative depletion by the end of 2008 is about 1.9 km³ (fig. 6; table 1).

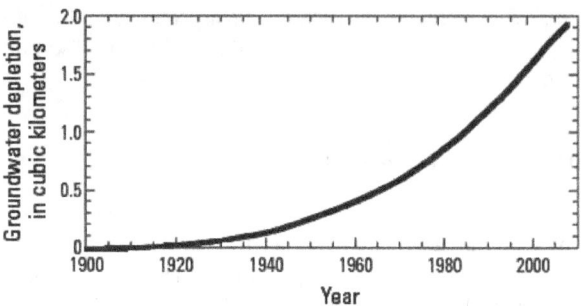

Figure 6. Cumulative groundwater depletion in the coastal plain aquifer system of Maryland and Delaware, 1900 through 2008.

New Jersey

The New Jersey coastal plain includes about 10,900 km² of the southeastern half of the State (figs. 1 and 2). The climate is humid and temperate (Ator and others, 2005). The average annual precipitation is about 114 cm/yr and evapotranspiration is about 57 cm/yr (Martin, 1998). The coastal plain aquifer system consists of a southeastward-thickening wedge of unconsolidated gravel, sand, silt, and clay, which thickens to over 2,000 m at the southern end of Cape May County (Martin, 1998). The six main confining units are composed mainly of clay and silt with minor amounts of sand (Martin, 1998). The hydrogeology is described in more detail by Zapecza (1989) and Ator and others (2005).

Withdrawals from the confined aquifers in New Jersey began in the late 1800s. By the 1990s large groundwater declines, some to more than 60 m below sea level, occurred in several locations in the State as the result of development of the groundwater system (Barlow, 2003, Box D). Groundwater withdrawals were less than 0.07 km³/yr in 1918, and pumpage steadily increased over the century. By 1980, nearly 80 percent of the potable water supply in the New Jersey coastal plain was from groundwater resources, and withdrawal rates had exceeded 0.5 km³/yr (Zapecza and others, 1987). It was estimated by Martin (1998, table 7) that a cumulative total of about 14.7 km³ of groundwater was pumped from the New Jersey coastal plain from 1896 to 1980. In the mid-1980s "Water Supply Critical Areas" were designated by the State, which mandated reduced withdrawals after 1988 (Barlow, 2003). Consequently, water levels rose in a number of areas—as much as 37 m between 1988 and 1993. Additional rises of up to 15 m were observed from 1993 to 1998 as pumpage rates decreased to approximately 0.3 km³/yr (Lacombe and Rosman, 2001; Barlow, 2003). From 1998 to 2003, water levels generally remained stable or rose, but in some areas water levels continued to decline as a result of pumping (dePaul and others, 2009). The hydrographs for numerous observation wells for 1978–2003 are presented by dePaul and others (2009); most show declining or stable levels since 1980, although some show notable rises.

A quasi-3D, transient, finite-difference model (Trescott, 1975; Leahy, 1982) for the coastal plain aquifer system in New Jersey was developed by Martin (1998). Confining units were not explicitly represented, so this modeling approach inherently ignores transient changes in storage in the confining units. An initial steady-state model was developed for predevelopment conditions (prior to 1895) and the transient model was developed for the period from 1896 through 1980. The transient model was divided into nine stress periods. The finite-difference grid included 29 rows, 51 columns, and 11 layers. Cell areas in the grid range from 16.2 km² in the northern and southwestern parts of the New Jersey coastal plain to 24.3 km² in the southeast. More details about the model are discussed by Martin (1998).

The calibrated model computed a water budget for 1896 through 1980 (Martin, 1998, table 12). Integrating these rates from 1900 through 1980 indicates that a total cumulative volume of 0.50 km³ of water was derived from depletion of storage in the New Jersey coastal plain aquifer system.

The method of Konikow and Neuzil (2007) was used to estimate the volume of water depleted from confining layers. Martin (1998) tested the sensitivity of the model to uncertainty in the assumed value of specific storage in the confining units. On that basis, a value of $S_s = 2 \times 10^{-5}$ m⁻¹ is assumed to be applicable for purposes of estimating groundwater depletion from the confining units. Simulated 1896 and 1978 (Martin, 1998, figs. 30–38 and 42–50) maps for the aquifers were used to compute head changes over the area; thickness maps of the confining units (Martin, 1998) were used to compute average thicknesses over the area. The calculated total volume of water removed from storage for the nine confining units between the years 1896 and 1978 is 0.71 km³. Because development was minor before the early 1900s and because of uncertainty in the estimate, the computed depletion is assumed to be representative for 1900–80. It is also assumed that the rate of depletion from confining units parallels the fractional rate of depletion from the aquifers. The total depletion through 1980 is about 1.2 km³.

Extrapolation through 2008 is based on the information on pumping rates and water-level changes in monitoring wells since 1980. On this basis, it is assumed that during 1981–87, relatively high withdrawal rates, water-level declines, and depletion continued at the average rate estimated for 1978–80. During 1988–97, withdrawals were reduced, water-levels generally rose, and depletion was reversed, yielding recovery of water in storage that balanced the total depletion estimated for 1981–87. During 1998–2008, water levels on the average were stable, and there was no net change in the volume in storage. The time rate of depletion thus estimated (fig. 7) indicates that the total depletion in the New Jersey coastal plain in both 2000 and 2008 was 1.2 km³ (table 1).

North Carolina

The Atlantic Coastal Plain in North Carolina includes an area of about 65,000 km² in the eastern part of the State

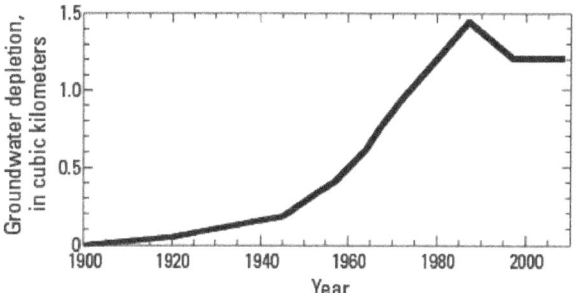

Figure 7. Cumulative groundwater depletion in the coastal plain aquifer system of New Jersey, 1900 through 2008.

(figs. 1 and 2). The climate is temperate and annual precipitation is about 100 to 140 cm/yr in North Carolina (Campbell and others, 2010). The coastal plain aquifer system provides a major source of water for municipal and domestic supply, as well as for industry and agriculture. Pumpage from the aquifer system has led to declines in groundwater levels, reduction of base flow to streams, and encroachment of saltwater in the coastal region (Giese and others, 1991). Winner and Coble (1996) provide a more detailed description of the hydrologic setting.

The aquifers and confining units consist of carbonate rocks, sand, silt, clay, and gravel and contain large volumes of high-quality groundwater (Campbell and others, 2010). This sequence of sediments gradually increases in thickness from the Fall Line (contact of the coastal plain sediments with the upland Piedmont crystalline rocks) to the Atlantic Coast and gently dips to the east. The hydrogeologic framework is described in more detail by Winner and Coble (1996), Lautier (2001), McFarland and Bruce (2006), and Gellici and Lautier (2010).

Groundwater development of deeper aquifers has led to declines in water levels since the early 1900s. Declines of up to 46 m have been observed near the city of Kinston. Three large cones of depression had developed by 1986, affecting more than 20 percent of the area in the North Carolina coastal plain aquifer system (Winner and Coble, 1996).

A quasi-3D transient groundwater-flow model was created for the entire coastal plain aquifer system in North Carolina (Giese and others, 1991), which did not explicitly simulate confining units. The 80-year simulation for 1900–80 indicated a cumulative depletion of 0.34 km³ from the aquifers. Extrapolation of withdrawals and storage changes indicate that the total net depletion in 2000 would be about 0.6 km³ from the aquifers. The additional depletion from confining units was estimated using the method of Konikow and Neuzil (2007) with the calculated head changes and an assumed value of specific storage of 8×10^{-5} m⁻¹. This approach indicates that total volume of water removed from storage from four confining units is about 0.7 km³. The total depletion for 1900–2000 is therefore about 1.3 km³.

A 3D transient groundwater-flow model was developed and calibrated (Coes and others, 2010) using MOD-

FLOW-2000 (Harbaugh and others, 2000) for a larger part of the Atlantic Coastal Plain—from central Georgia to central Virginia—that included North Carolina. The model included 16 layers to represent the series of aquifers and confining units. The model used a regular grid of 130 rows and 275 columns of cells that are about 3.2 km on a side. The active area of the grid encompasses about 207,000 km². The model simulated groundwater flow from 1900 (assumed to represent predevelopment conditions) to the end of 2003—a 104-year simulation period. Variable-length time periods of constant pumpage (stress periods) were used, ranging from 10-year stress periods through 1978 to 1-year stress periods during the final 8 years of the simulation period. More details about the model conceptualization and calibration are presented by Coes and others (2010).

The northern part of the North Carolina Coastal Plain is also included in a recent Virginia model (Heywood and Pope, 2009), and a small southern part of the North Carolina Coastal Plain is also included in a recent South Carolina model (Petkewich and Campbell, 2007). For purposes of estimating the total depletion in the United States, and to avoid double counting of depletion in parts of North Carolina that are included in the other models, only the additional depletion in North Carolina from the model results for the central part of the State are estimated here (Coes and others, 2010). The area not covered by models for adjacent States includes two of the three major cones of depression in North Carolina, two of the six major cones of depression in the modeled area of Coes and others (2010), and about one-third of the total groundwater withdrawals. Therefore, it is assumed that the total depletion in the separate North Carolina area equals 33 percent of the total net depletion computed by the model of the larger area.

The water budget computed by the calibrated transient model indicates that a cumulative volume of 3.6 km³ was removed from storage in the aquifers and confining units through 2000 and that the groundwater depletion increased to 3.8 km³ at the end of 2003 (Coes and others, 2010). Extrapolating through 2008 using the average rate calculated during the final 5 years of the model simulation period indicates that cumulative depletion is about 4.9 km³ by 2008 for the entire modeled area. Attributing 33 percent of that to the part of North Carolina not covered by other models indicates that the cumulative depletion was 1.2 km³ and 1.6 km³ in 2000 and 2008, respectively (table 1). The former agrees closely with the estimate based on the earlier model (Giese and others, 1991) and the related estimate of confining layer depletion. The long-term history of cumulative depletion is plotted in figure 8.

South Carolina

The aquifers and confining units in the Atlantic Coastal Plain of South Carolina and adjacent parts of Georgia and North Carolina consist of sand, silt, clay, and limestone (Aucott, 1996) (figs. 1 and 2). The area has a temperate climate and precipitation averages about 120 cm/yr.

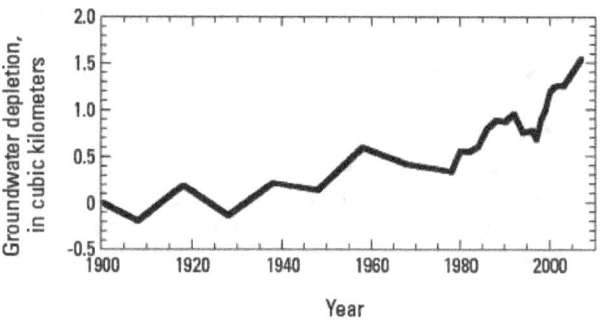

Figure 8.   Cumulative groundwater depletion in the coastal plain aquifer system of North Carolina, 1900 through 2008.

As described by Petkewich and Campbell (2007), the coastal plain sediments consist of a wedge-shaped accumulation of unconsolidated to poorly consolidated clay, silt, sand, and limestone overlying metamorphic, igneous, and sedimentary rocks (Miller, 1986; Aucott, 1996). This sedimentary sequence gradually increases in thickness from the Fall Line to the Atlantic Coast. In South Carolina, the thickness of the coastal plain sediments ranges from about 300 m near the North Carolina border to about 1,400 m near the Georgia border. The hydrogeologic framework is described in more detail by Aucott (1996), McFarland and Bruce (2006), and Gellici and Lautier (2010).

Declines in water levels have been observed in the coastal plain aquifer system in South Carolina since the early 1930s, as depicted in figure 9. Several large cones of depression existed by 2000. The temporal change in groundwater withdrawals during the 20th century has been estimated by Petkewich and Campbell (2007, fig. 5).

A transient 3D groundwater-flow model of the area was developed and calibrated by Petkewich and Campbell (2007) using MODFLOW-2000 (Harbaugh and others, 2000). The system was vertically discretized into nine model layers to include five aquifers and four intervening confining units. The model assumed steady-state predevelopment conditions existed in 1900 and simulated transient development and effects through 2004. In the model, the total cumulative specified well withdrawals for 1900 through the end of 2000 equaled 17.1 km³ (and equaled 19.1 km³ through the end of the simulation in 2004). The model used a variably spaced grid to facilitate simulating steep cones of depression in their area of interest around Mount Pleasant and Charleston, South Carolina. Cell size varied from 305 m on a side near Mount Pleasant to a maximum of 3,050 m on a side at model boundaries (Petkewich and Campbell, 2007). The best fit calibration required specific storage values that were equal to the minimum value allowed (8.2×10^{-6} m^{-1}) for all layers except the surficial aquifer (Petkewich and Campbell, 2007). The model used the same values of specific storage for the aquifers and the clayey confining units, so may be underestimating the value of specific storage in those confining units. In a larger regional coastal plain model that included South Carolina, Coes and others (2010) similarly estimated the value

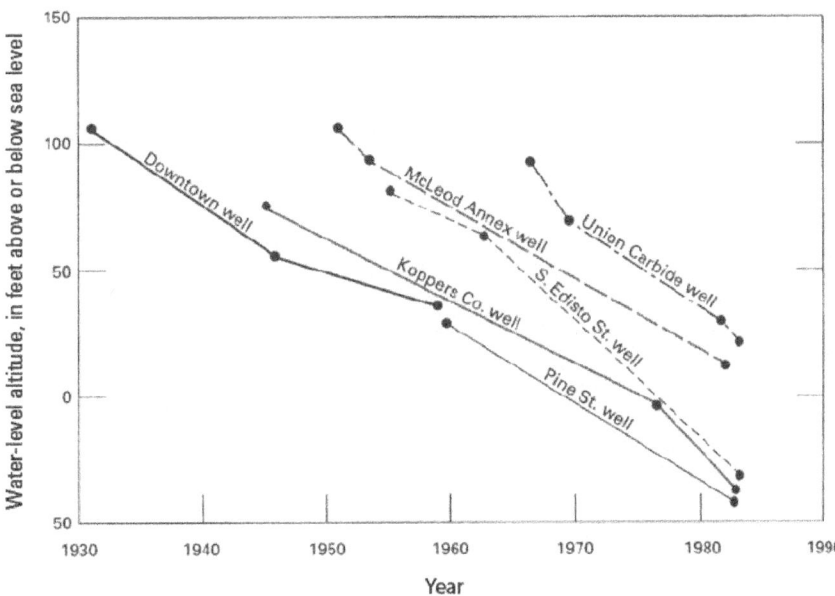

Figure 9. Water-level declines for selected wells in the Middendorf aquifer near Florence, South Carolina (from Aucott, 1996, as modified from Aucott and Speiran, 1985).

of specific storage for all aquifer and confining unit layers beneath the surficial layer as 4.9×10^{-6} m^{-1}.

The water budget computed by the calibrated transient model indicated that a cumulative volume of 2.8 km³ was removed from storage in the aquifers and confining units through 2000 (Petkewich and Campbell, 2007). From predevelopment through 2000 almost 17 percent of the water withdrawn through wells was derived from storage depletion. The computed groundwater depletion increased to 3.1 km³ after four more years (through 2004). Assuming that the 2003–04 rate of 0.035 km³/yr applies for the following four years lets us extrapolate that the total depletion by 2008 is 3.2 km³ (table 1). The estimated growth in cumulative depletion during 1900–2008 is shown in figure 10.

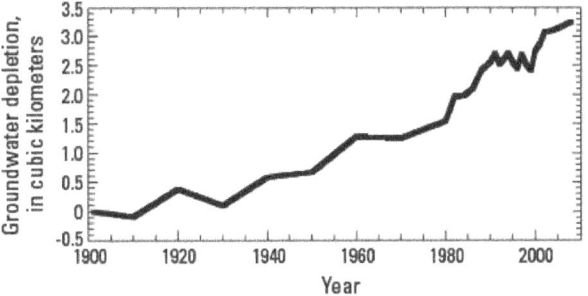

Figure 10. Cumulative groundwater depletion in the coastal plain aquifer system of South Carolina, 1900 through 2008.

Virginia

The Atlantic Coastal Plain aquifer system includes approximately 34,000 km² of eastern Virginia (Meng and Harsh, 1988) (figs. 1 and 2). The aquifer system consists of an eastward-thickening sedimentary wedge atop a basement surface that slopes gently eastward and is composed of unconsolidated sedimentary aquifers separated by clayey confining units. The maximum thickness of the sediments in the study area is over 1,800 m (Meng and Harsh, 1988). The hydrogeologic framework is described in detail by Meng and Harsh (1988) and McFarland and Bruce (2006).

The climate in the coastal plain region of Virginia is temperate. The average annual precipitation is about 109 cm/yr, and about 55 cm/yr of the precipitation is estimated to be lost from the groundwater system as evapotranspiration from vegetation (Harsh and Laczniak, 1990).

Groundwater from the coastal plain aquifer system is an important source of municipal, domestic, industrial, and agricultural supply (Harsh and Laczniak, 1990). Groundwater use from the confined aquifers began in Virginia by the late 1800s, and the estimated annual discharge from flowing wells in the study area ranged from 0.006 to 0.014 km³/yr during the water years 1891 to 1945. Flowing wells were a significant source of supply until 1935 when water levels in deeper confined wells fell below land surface (Harsh and Laczniak, 1990). Withdrawals significantly increased in the State after 1955 to approximately 0.14 km³/yr by 1980. Water levels were observed to decline as much as 60 m.

A total of 4.5 km³ of groundwater was pumped from the Virginia coastal plain aquifer system from 1891 until 1980 (Harsh and Laczniak, 1990). More recent withdrawal data indicate that during 1992 withdrawals totaled approximately 0.13 km³/yr, during a drought year in 2002 totaled about 0.19 km³/yr, and during 2003 (after the drought ended) totaled about 0.17 km³/yr (McFarland and Bruce, 2006). Examination of several representative observation wells in the Virginia coastal plain aquifer system (for example, see *http://groundwaterwatch.usgs.gov/AWLSites.asp?S=363722077014601*) indicates that water levels have continued to decline steadily since 1980 through 2009. These declines indicate that water was still being removed from storage at approximately the same rate as during 1978–80.

A 3D transient model of the groundwater flow system in the coastal plain in Virginia, and small adjacent areas in North Carolina and Maryland, was developed and calibrated by Heywood and Pope (2009) using the SEAWAT model (Guo and Langevin, 2002). The finite-difference model grid includes 134 rows, 96 columns, and 60 layers, representing distinct aquifers and confining units (Heywood and Pope, 2009). The grid spacing is variable, ranging from 1.6 to 16.0 km on a side. The 113-year historical transient simulation of 1891–2003 was discretized into 34 stress periods of varying length—using 1-year stress periods for 1982–2003 and longer stress periods for earlier times. An initial steady-state stress period represented predevelopment conditions prior to 1891. Values of specific storage of confining units used by Heywood and Pope (2009) ranged from 3.3×10^{-6} m^{-1} to 2.3×10^{-4} m^{-1}. More details on hydraulic properties, stresses, and boundary conditions are presented by Heywood and Pope (2009). This model was further updated and refined to extend the simulation period through 2008 by incorporating new withdrawal, recharge, boundary condition, and observation data for 2004–08 (J.P. Pope and J.R. Eggleston, written commun., 2010).

The volumetric budgets computed by the updated model indicate a cumulative depletion from aquifers and confining units by 2000 of about 2.7 km^3 and by 2008 of about 4.8 km^3. The data show that of the total 2008 withdrawals of about 0.194 km^3, approximately 7 percent is attributable to withdrawals in Maryland. Assuming that 7 percent of depletion is also attributable to Maryland, only 93 percent of the model-computed depletion is included in the summation for Virginia to avoid double-counting the Maryland depletion, which was computed separately on the basis of other model studies that included the same as in the Virginia model. On this basis, the estimated history of depletion in Virginia (fig. 11) indicates that since 1900 the cumulative depletion in 2000 is 2.5 km^3 and by 2008 is 4.5 km^3 (table 1).

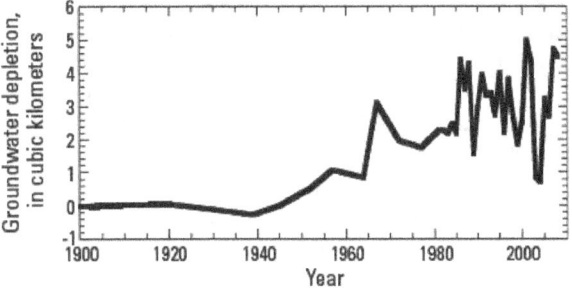

Figure 11.   Cumulative groundwater depletion in the coastal plain aquifer system of Virginia, 1900 through 2008.

Atlantic Coastal Plain: Total

The Atlantic Coastal Plain extends from Long Island, New York, southward to northeastern Florida (dePaul and others, 2008). The area is bounded on the west by the Fall Line and on the east by the Atlantic Ocean and encompasses an area of approximately 270,000 km^2. The Atlantic Coastal Plain is underlain by a seaward-dipping wedge of clay, silt, sand, gravel, and carbonate rocks that thicken seaward from a featheredge at the Fall Line to approximately 3,000 m at Cape Hatteras, North Carolina. This sedimentary wedge forms a complex groundwater system in which the unconsolidated sands and gravels and the openings in consolidated carbonate rocks function as aquifers, and the silts and clays function as confining units. Depletion in the Atlantic Coastal Plain was estimated in seven separate subareas, as described above. Integrating these estimates yields a total cumulative depletion since 1900 (fig. 12) of about 14.4 km^3 in 2000 and 17.2 km^3 in 2008 (table 1).

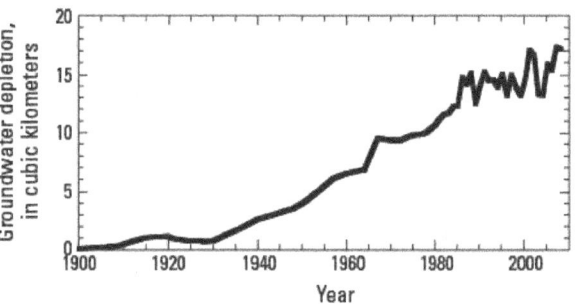

Figure 12.   Cumulative groundwater depletion in the Atlantic Coastal Plain, 1900 through 2008.

Gulf Coastal Plain

Coastal Lowlands of Alabama, Florida, Louisiana, and Mississippi

The coastal lowlands aquifer system adjacent to the Gulf Coast in Alabama, Florida, Louisiana, and Mississippi covers a total area of 188,000 km^2, including 152,000 km^2 on land and 37,000 km^2 in adjacent offshore areas (see Martin and Whiteman, 1999, fig. 1) (figs. 1 and 2). The area is characterized by long, hot, humid summers and relatively short, mild winters (Martin and Whiteman, 1999). Precipitation averages about 147 cm/yr but exceeds 162 cm/yr near the coastline.

The aquifer system consists of complexly interbedded sands, gravels, silts, and clays of Oligocene age and younger (Martin and Whiteman, 1989; Martin and Whiteman, 1999). Based on analysis of borehole geophysical data and the vertical distribution of hydraulic head, the thick sedimentary sequence of the Coastal Lowlands aquifer system was subdivided into five regional permeable zones by Weiss and Williamson (1985). Using this subdivision, a quasi-3D, transient, six-layer groundwater-flow model of the Coastal Lowlands aquifer system in Alabama, Florida, Louisiana, and Mississippi was developed by Martin and Whiteman (1989, 1999) using MODFLOW (McDonald and Harbaugh, 1988). Each layer is discretized into a uniformly spaced grid of 78 rows and 70 columns consisting of cells measuring 8 km on a side. Temporally, the model is divided into nine stress periods between 1898 and 1987. The first stress period represents an initial steady-state simulation under predevelopment conditions. Periods 1 through 3 are transient simulations lasting 20 years each, and periods 4 through 9 are transient simulations representing 5 years each.

Groundwater withdrawals within the study area have resulted in the formation of several local cones of depression around the major pumping centers. Since development began in the early 20th century, drawdown in excess of 30 m has occurred near the cities of Lake Charles and Baton Rouge, Louisiana, as well as in parts of southern Mississippi (Martin and Whiteman, 1999). Declining water levels have also been observed near New Orleans, Louisiana (Dial and Tomaszewski, 1988; Dial and Sumner, 1989). Pumpage has also resulted in land-surface subsidence in the Baton Rouge area, a consequence of a reduction in groundwater storage and compaction of dehydrated clays (Wintz and others, 1970).

Martin and Whiteman (1999) discuss the model calibration process and results in detail. The model-calculated water budgets indicate that although reduction of groundwater storage accounts for only 1 percent of total flow into or out of the Coastal Lowlands aquifer system in Alabama, Florida, Louisiana, and Mississippi in 1987 (Martin and Whiteman, 1999, p. 28), the volume of water derived from storage reduction between 1898 and 1987 is substantial. Since 1958, storage losses have accounted for approximately 15 percent of total pumpage. A cumulative volume of 31.2 km³ was derived from a reduction in groundwater storage in the Coastal Lowlands aquifer system in Alabama, Florida, Louisiana, and Mississippi between 1898 and 1987 (Martin and Whiteman, 1999, p. 33). Because the model did not simulate changes in storage within confining units, it is likely that the calculated cumulative depletion represents an underestimate of the actual total depletion.

To partly offset the model limitation of not simulating confining layer storage, an estimate of depletion from confining layers is made using the method of Konikow and Neuzil (2007). The inelastic specific storage (S_s) in clay units in three different permeable zones are 2.8×10^{-4} m^{-1}, 2.6×10^{-4} m^{-1}, and 2.6×10^{-5} m^{-1} (Ryder and Ardis, 2002). This analysis assumes an effective average value close to the lower end of the range of $S_s = 3.3\times10^{-5}$ m^{-1}. Changes in head were derived from maps presented by Williamson and Grubb (2001). The results indicated an additional depletion of 5.4 km³ through 1987. It is assumed that the rate of growth of confining layer depletion parallels that of the depletion from the aquifers, and is included in the estimated historical growth of cumulative groundwater depletion (fig. 13).

Hydrographs showing long-term water-level records from 15 deep observation wells in the Baton Rouge, Louisiana, area are available from the U.S. Geological Survey at:

http://la.water.usgs.gov/WellsByAquifer.asp?Aquifer=2,000-foot_Sand_of_Baton_Rouge. Most of these hydrographic records show relatively steep water-level declines prior to 1987, with several showing some water-level recoveries during the early to mid-1980s. After 1987, a few wells show no overall change through 2010, several show continued declines at much lower rates, and several show continued declines at almost the same rate as prior to 1987. On the whole, it is clear that depletion has continued during 1988–2008. The depletion curve is extended from 1987 by assuming that, on the average, depletion during 1988–2008 continued at half the rate observed during the 15-year period from 1972 through 1987 (when depletion averaged about 0.18 km³/yr). On this basis, cumulative depletion in 2000 is 37.8 km³ and in 2008 is 38.5 km³ (table 1).

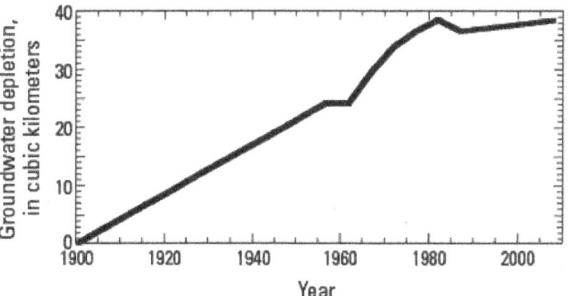

Figure 13. Cumulative groundwater depletion in the coastal lowlands of Alabama, Florida, Louisiana, and Mississippi, 1900 through 2008.

Houston Area and Northern Part of Texas Gulf Coast

The northern part of the Gulf Coast aquifer system in southeastern Texas includes an area of approximately 65,000 km² surrounding the Beaumont and Houston metropolitan areas (figs. 1 and 2). The area is located within the gently sloping Gulf Coastal Plain of southeastern Texas. The climate in the study area is characterized as humid subtropical, with a mean annual temperature of 20 °C and average annual precipitation of 120 cm. Surface-water hydrology within the study area is dominated by six major rivers: the Brazos, Colorado, Lavaca, and Sabine Rivers, which drain into the Gulf of Mexico; and the San Jacinto and Trinity Rivers, which drain into Galveston Bay (Kasmarek and Robinson, 2004).

The Gulf Coastal Plain in Texas is underlain by a thick sequence of Tertiary and Quaternary clays, silts, sands, and gravels. Beds dip southeast toward the Gulf of Mexico and thicken in that direction. A detailed description of the regional hydrogeology is presented by Baker (1979).

Historically, pumpage from aquifers has supplied nearly all of the water used for industrial, municipal, agricultural, and commercial purposes in the region. The first well in the Gulf Coast aquifer system was drilled in 1886 in the city of

Houston. By 1905, 65 wells in the Chicot and Evangeline aquifers were in production. Average withdrawals rapidly increased, from 4.2×10^4 m³/d in 1906 to 9.3×10^4 m³/d in 1935 and 1.0×10^5 m³/d in 1941 (Kasmarek and Robinson, 2004, p. 37). Pumping rates nearly doubled in the 1940s and doubled again during the 1950s before beginning to level off in the late 1960s (Ryder and Ardis, 2002).

Concern about the adverse effects of groundwater withdrawals along the Texas Gulf Coast region has led to the establishment of groundwater conservation groups, such as the Harris-Galveston Subsidence District (HGSD). The creation of the HGSD in 1975 has helped to further curb groundwater withdrawals, and regulatory action has led to decreasing water-usage trends in the 1980s and 1990s. Groundwater withdrawals in the Houston-Galveston area in 1996 were 1.8×10^6 m³/d, down from 1.9×10^6 m³/d in 1990 (Kasmarek and Robinson, 2004, p. 37). Meanwhile, withdrawals have been increasing in the coastal rice-irrigation area and in the Evadale-Beaumont area. Irrigation withdrawals in Wharton County were about 6.9×10^5 m³/d in 2000, up from 4.9×10^5 m³/d in 1995. Withdrawals in the Evadale-Beaumont area increased from a combined 9.1×10^4 m³/d in 1977 to 1.7×10^5 m³/d in 2000 (Kasmarek and Robinson, 2004, p. 37). Prolonged heavy withdrawals have resulted in potentiometric-surface declines in the Chicot, Evangeline, and Jasper aquifers (as much as 110 m of drawdown) and land-surface subsidence from depressurization and compaction of clay layers interbedded in the aquifer sediments (Kasmarek and Robinson, 2004).

A 3D transient groundwater-flow model for the northern part of the Gulf Coast aquifer system in Texas was developed by Kasmarek and Robinson (2004). The model uses MODFLOW96 (Harbaugh and McDonald, 1996) and the Interbed-Storage Package (Leake and Prudic, 1991) to simulate flow conditions and land-surface subsidence due to the release of water from storage in the clays of the Chicot and Evangeline aquifers. The model consists of four layers, representing the Chicot aquifer, the Evangeline aquifer, the Burkeville confining unit, and the Jasper aquifer. Each model layer is discretized into a uniformly spaced grid of 137 rows and 245 columns consisting of cells measuring 1.6 km on each side. Temporally, the model is discretized into 69 stress periods to represent 1891 through 2000. The first stress period represents an initial steady-state simulation under predevelopment conditions. The 68 transient stress periods vary in duration, with the longest period (period 3) lasting 30 years and the shortest ones (periods 16, 29, and 46) lasting 28 days each (Kasmarek and Robinson, 2004).

Initial assumptions of storage properties for the Chicot and Evangeline aquifers were based on values reported in Carr and others (1985) and Kasmarek and Strom (2002). Storativity values ranged from 4×10^{-4} to 0.1 in the Chicot aquifer, and from 5×10^{-4} to 0.1 in the Evangeline aquifer. These value ranges reflect subsurface conditions that range from confined to unconfined. The storativity of sands in the Burkeville confining unit was estimated as 3×10^{-7} m^{-1} times the sand layer thickness. The specific storage value of 3×10^{-7} m^{-1} is represen-

tative of confined aquifers (Lohman, 1972). This calculation yields a range of storativity values from 1×10^{-5} to 0.05 for sands in the Burkeville confining unit. Storativity values in the Jasper aquifer are from Wesselman (1967) and Strom and others (2003) and range from 2×10^{-5} to 0.2.

Initial inelastic storativity values for the interbedded clays in the Chicot and Evangeline aquifers were computed by multiplying the clay layer thickness by values of inelastic clay-specific storage from Meyer and Carr (1979) (2.7×10^{-5} m^{-1} for the Chicot aquifer and 1.4×10^{-6} m^{-1} for the Evangeline aquifer). Elastic clay storativity was assumed to be two orders of magnitude lower than inelastic clay storativity and thus was computed by multiplying inelastic clay storativity values by 0.01 (Kasmarek and Robinson, 2004, p. 46). During calibration, slight adjustments were made to the storage properties of the aquifers and interbedded clays. A more detailed description of the groundwater-flow model and calibration procedure are provided by Kasmarek and Robinson (2004).

Approximately 63 km³ of groundwater were pumped from the northern part of the Gulf Coast aquifer system in Texas between 1891 and 2000. The simulation results for the model indicate that approximately 18.1 km³ (about 29 percent of the total pumpage) was derived from a reduction in aquifer storage during the 20th century (Kasmarek and Robinson, 2004). In addition, an estimated volume of 10.8 km³ was derived from storage losses in the interbedded clays of the Chicot and Evangeline aquifers, a value that is supported by an independent estimate of the volume of land-surface subsidence (10.5 ±0.5 km³). The estimated total groundwater depletion from the northern part of the Gulf Coast aquifer system in Texas during the 20th century is 28.9 km³. Extrapolation of the rate calculated for 1997–2000 (0.28 km³/yr) through 2008 indicates a total depletion volume of about 31.1 km³ (table 1). The estimated cumulative change in depletion during 1900–2008 is plotted in figure 14.

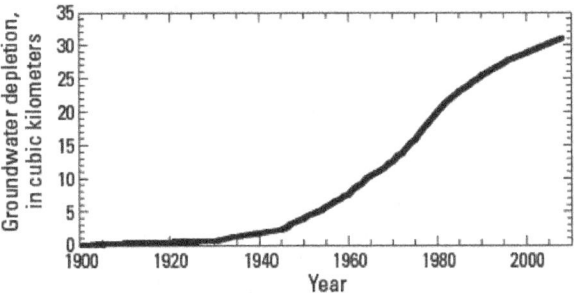

Figure 14. Cumulative groundwater depletion in the northern part of the Texas Gulf Coastal Plain, 1900 through 2008.

As an independent cross-check of the model-calculated volume of water released from storage in the clay layers (10.8 km³), an estimate of the volume of land-surface subsidence in the Houston-Galveston area was made using GIS tools. Because land-surface subsidence is caused by the dewatering and compaction of clays, these two volumes should closely coincide. A contour map of estimated subsidence from 1906 through 2000 prepared by the HGSD (*http://www.hgsubsidence.org/about/subsidence/land-surface-subsidence.html*) was discretized into a uniform grid of 166 rows and 215 columns consisting of cells measuring 1.6 km on each side. Summing the subsidence volume calculated for each cell yields an estimated total subsidence volume of 10.5 km³. Because of uncertainty and errors in the position, extrapolation, and interpolation of subsidence contours, this estimate of subsidence volume probably has an uncertainty of about ±0.5 km³. Nevertheless, the estimated value is in very good agreement with the estimate of 10.8 km³ derived from the model by Kasmarek and Robinson (2004). The difference of less than 3 percent provides good support for the quality of the model calibration and its reliability.

Central Part of Gulf Coast Aquifer System in Texas

The central part of the Gulf Coast aquifer system in Texas covers an area of approximately 60,000 km² and includes all or part of 29 counties (figs. 1 and 2). Considerable withdrawals have impacted the potentiometric surface in the Chicot, Evangeline, and Jasper aquifers. The area is located within the gently sloping Gulf Coastal Plain of southeastern Texas. Mean annual precipitation ranges from 58 cm in the southwest to 140 cm in the northeast.

The Gulf Coastal Plain in Texas is underlain by a thick sequence of Tertiary and Quaternary clays, silts, sands, and gravels. Beds dip eastward toward the Gulf of Mexico and thicken in that direction. A more detailed description of the regional hydrogeology may be found in Baker (1979; 1986). The Tertiary and Quaternary sediments are divided into five hydrogeologic units. From the land surface downward, these are the Chicot aquifer, the Evangeline aquifer, the Burkeville confining unit, the Jasper aquifer, and the Catahoula confining unit.

Although the first wells were drilled prior to 1900, pumping rates in the area remained fairly low until the middle of the 20th century (Groschen, 1985). Groundwater withdrawals are primarily used for agricultural, municipal, and industrial use. A history of heavy groundwater withdrawals has led to the formation of a regional cone of depression centered near the city of Kingsville. Localized drawdown of approximately 76 m in this area has been observed historically (Groschen, 1985); by 1999, drawdown near Kingsville exceeded 46 m (Chowdhury and others, 2004). Water levels throughout much of the study area have been declining, and drawdown of as much as 15 m has been observed in Jackson and Matagorda Counties (Chowdhury and others, 2004).

Annual groundwater pumpage has generally been decreasing since 1980, from about 2.1×10⁶ m³/d in 1980 to about 1.5×10⁶ m³/d in 1999 (Chowdhury and others, 2004, fig. 16). Declining withdrawals have corresponded to recovery of water levels in parts of the study area (Chowdhury and others, 2004).

A 3D, transient groundwater-flow model in the central part of the Gulf Coast aquifer system in Texas was developed by Waterstone Environmental Hydrology and Engineering, Inc. (2003) in cooperation with the Texas Water Development Board (TWDB) as part of the TWDB Ground-water Availability Modeling (GAM) program. The model was recalibrated using TWDB estimates of pumpage rates and distribution (Chowdhury and others, 2004). The model uses MODFLOW96 (Harbaugh and McDonald, 1996) to simulate flow conditions from 1920 (assumed to be representative of predevelopment conditions) to 1999.

The model consists of four layers, representing the Chicot aquifer, the Evangeline aquifer, the Burkeville confining unit, and the Jasper aquifer. Each layer is discretized into a uniformly spaced grid of 177 rows and 269 columns, which consist of cells measuring 1.6 km on each side. The model has a total of 56,736 active cells. Temporally, the model is discretized into 87 stress periods between 1920 and 1999. The first stress period represents an initial steady-state simulation under predevelopment conditions. The 86 transient stress periods vary in duration, with the longest period (period 2) lasting 40 years (for 1940–80) and the shortest periods lasting 28 days each. For steady-state conditions, the model was calibrated to reproduce mean annual winter water levels from 1920 through 1940. During this period, no significant pumping occurred; thus, changes in the water levels of the aquifers are assumed to be negligible.

Calibrated values of specific storage range from 3×10^{-6} m⁻¹ to 3×10^{-5} m⁻¹. The specific yield values used in the model (0.01 to 0.005) represent semi-confined conditions rather than unconfined conditions, and therefore are lower than typical specific yield values in unconfined aquifers (Chowdhury and others, 2004, p. 52). Chowdhury and others (2004) present a more detailed description of the calibration procedure and results.

It was estimated that a cumulative volume of 40 km³ of groundwater was pumped from the central part of the Gulf Coast aquifer system in Texas between 1920 and 1999, and this was specified in the model with appropriate spatial and temporal pumping distributions (Waterstone Environmental Hydrology and Engineering, Inc., 2003; Chowdhury and others, 2004). The water budget calculated by the model indicates that 4.6 km³, or about 11 percent of total pumpage, was derived from a reduction in groundwater storage in aquifers and one confining unit. Assuming that the last calculated rate of depletion (0.156 km³/yr during 1997–99) also applies to 2000, the total depletion in 2000 would be 4.8 km³. Because no data are yet available to establish water-level trends during 2001–08, and recognizing that the recent short-term increase in depletion follows a longer-term trend of recovery, it is conservatively assumed that there is no change in depletion volume after 2000 (table 1). The resulting time rate of cumulative depletion is plotted in figure 15.

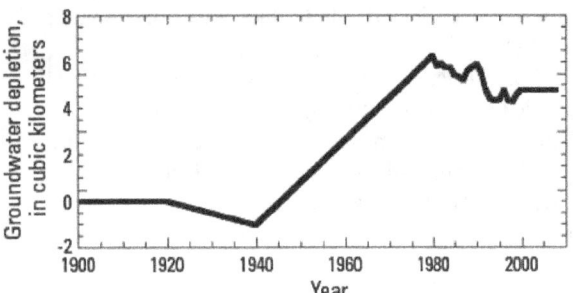

Figure 15. Cumulative groundwater depletion in the central part of the Texas Gulf Coastal Plain, 1900 through 2008.

Winter Garden Area, Southern Part of Texas Gulf Coast

The Winter Garden area, an agricultural area in southern Texas, covers approximately 30,500 km^2 (Klemt and others, 1976) (figs. 1 and 2). The climate is subtropical and semiarid. Mean annual precipitation in the Winter Garden area ranges from 53 to 74 cm. The Winter Garden area is located within the Texas coastal uplands aquifer system (Grubb, 1998). More detailed discussions, including descriptions of all stratigraphic and hydrogeologic units in the Winter Garden area, may be found in Klemt and others (1976), McCoy (1991), and Ryder and Ardis (2002).

The first irrigation well in the area was drilled in 1884 in Dimmit County (Klemt and others, 1976). Early wells were flowing wells, with artesian heads of as much as 12 m above the land surface (Ryder and Ardis, 2002, p. 40). The lower Claiborne-upper Wilcox aquifer (also known as the Carrizo-Wilcox aquifer) has been intensively pumped for large-scale irrigation of vegetables and other food crops since the early 1900s. By 1929, flow to the Carrizo Springs had ceased (McCoy, 1991; Ryder and Ardis, 2002). In 1950, a widespread drought led to a drastic increase in groundwater withdrawals. Withdrawals jumped from 3.0×10^5 m^3/d in 1950 to about 8.7×10^5 m^3/d in 1965 (Grubb, 1998). Since 1965, withdrawals have been more stable, varying from 8.3×10^5 to 1.1×10^6 m^3/d between 1965 and 1990 (Grubb, 1998).

Prolonged heavy withdrawals from the lower Claiborne-upper Wilcox aquifer have led to the formation of a large cone of depression in the Winter Garden area, with a maximum drawdown of over 76 m occurring in Zavala and Dimmit Counties. Seven counties have drawdown in excess of 30 m.

A map of the decline in the potentiometric surface of the lower Claiborne-upper Wilcox aquifer between predevelopment and 1982 (Ryder and Ardis, 2002) provides the basis for estimating the volume of groundwater removed from storage in the aquifer and overlying confining unit during this time period. Information from the map was supplemented by data from several additional sources (Klemt and others, 1976; McCoy, 1991; Grubb, 1998).

The potentiometric surface data were analyzed using GIS tools to assess the spatial distribution of water-level declines.

The declines were integrated with estimates of storage properties and area to estimate depletion from aquifers. In the outcrop area of the lower Claiborne-upper Wilcox aquifer, the aquifer is assumed to be under unconfined conditions and a specific yield value of 0.25 was assumed. Elsewhere, where the aquifer is under confined conditions, a storage coefficient value of 0.0005 was assumed. The results indicate that a total between 4.5 and 13.0 km^3 of groundwater have been removed from storage in the lower Claiborne-upper Wilcox aquifer between predevelopment and 1982, with a median value of 8.7 km^3.

An estimate of the total depletion from the lower Claiborne confining unit was made using the method described by Konikow and Neuzil (2007). These calculations indicate that an additional 0.1–0.8 km^3 of groundwater, with a median value of 0.4 km^3, has been removed from storage in the overlying confining unit. Combining the median values, a total volume of 9.1 km^3 of groundwater has been removed from storage between predevelopment and 1982.

The long-term (1929–86) rate of water-level decline in a representative well hydrograph from well HZ-77-42-801 in the Winter Garden area (Grubb, 1998, fig. 24) can be used as a surrogate for the rate of depletion during that time. The record would also indicate no significant depletion prior to 1932. If the total water-level decline of about 32.6 m in 1982 is assumed to represent 100 percent, then, for example, the decline of about 31.4 m in 1968 would correspond to 96.3 percent of the total decline through 1982. This decline corresponds to a rate of depletion during 1968–82 of about 0.34 km^3 over 14 years, or 0.0243 km^3/yr.

During 1990–2000, water-level declines predominated over water-level rises in the area (Boghici, 2008). Long-term records from a water-supply well in Angelina County show a fairly steady rate of decline from the late 1940s through the early 2000s—with a total decline of more than 125 m (Boghici, 2008, fig. 4-9). These records provide a basis for assuming that the low depletion rate during 1968–82 also applies during 1983–2000. By extrapolation, it is estimated that the total depletion during the 20th century was approximately 9.5 km^3. Assuming more conservatively that depletion continued during 2001–2008 at just half the previous rate, further extrapolation indicates a total depletion of 9.6 km^3 in 2008 (fig. 16; table 1).

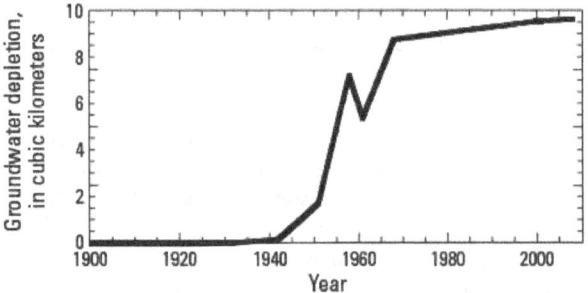

Figure 16. Cumulative groundwater depletion in the Winter Garden area in the southern part of the Texas Gulf Coastal Plain, 1900 through 2008.

Mississippi Embayment of the Gulf Coastal Plain

The Gulf Coastal Plain regional aquifer system has been divided into three areas: the Mississippi embayment, the coastal lowlands, and the Texas coastal uplands (Williamson and Grubb, 2001) (figs. 1 and 2). The Mississippi embayment aquifer system is comprised of six aquifers and three confining units (Grubb, 1986). It encompasses an area of about 202,000 km[2] in parts of eight States in the south-central United States. The climate of the embayment is moderate with a mean annual precipitation of 122 cm in the north to 142 cm in the south; precipitation is distributed fairly evenly throughout the year (Clark and Hart, 2009).

The aquifer units in the Mississippi embayment are generally formed of massive sand beds separated by extensive clay beds. The uppermost of these units is the Mississippi River Valley alluvial aquifer, which exists at land surface and covers much of the embayment area within the Mississippi alluvial plain (Clark and Hart, 2009). One of the next most widely used aquifers is the middle Claiborne aquifer, which, in some areas, lies a hundred or more meters beneath land surface. The hydrogeologic framework is described in more detail by Williamson and Grubb (2001) and Clark and Hart (2009). Decades of pumping from the alluvial aquifer for irrigation and from the middle Claiborne aquifer for industry and public water supply have affected groundwater levels throughout the northern Mississippi embayment in Arkansas, Louisiana, Mississippi, and Tennessee. The greatest losses in groundwater storage occur in the Mississippi River Valley alluvial aquifer, especially in Arkansas.

The first large-scale development in the Mississippi embayment study area began in Memphis, Tennessee, around 1886. Substantial development began in other parts of the Mississippi embayment area, such as southeast Arkansas and Jackson, Mississippi, in the 1920s. Groundwater withdrawals derived from the alluvial aquifer are primarily used for irrigation of rice or other crops and for fish farming. Withdrawals for rice irrigation began in Arkansas around 1904, but the earliest records of significant withdrawals began in about 1910 in the Grand Prairie region of Arkansas. Observable water-level declines occurred by the late 1920s (Mahon and Ludwig, 1990). From about 1915 through the early 1940s, withdrawal rates averaged about 0.25 km[3]/yr (Grubb, 1998).

There was a significant increase in rice production in 1942, and withdrawals reached nearly 2.2 km[3]/yr by 1954. This withdrawal rate remained constant until the 1970s, when production increased again during the early 1980s to early 1990s and withdrawal rates increased to as much as 6.9 km[3]/yr (Grubb, 1998). Groundwater withdrawals have increased 132 percent in the agricultural areas of Arkansas from 1985 to 2000. Approximately 11 km[3]/yr of groundwater was pumped in 2000 to meet irrigation requirements in Arkansas, Louisiana, and Mississippi (Hutson and others, 2004). Groundwater withdrawals for agriculture have caused water-level declines in the alluvial aquifer in Arkansas of at least 12 m in 40 years (Schrader, 2001) while withdrawals from confined aquifers in

Arkansas have resulted in declines of more than 110 m since the 1920s (Scheiderer and Freiwald, 2006). The area includes about 70,000 wells (Clark and Hart, 2009).

A 3D, transient simulation model of the Mississippi embayment regional aquifer was developed and calibrated by Clark and Hart (2009) using the MODFLOW-2005 model (Harbaugh, 2005). The finite-difference grid consists of 414 rows, 397 columns, and 13 layers. Each model cell is 2.59 km[2] with varying thickness by cell and by layer. The model simulates 137 years (1870–2007) of groundwater flow and head changes using 69 stress periods. The first stress period is simulated as steady state to represent predevelopment conditions. The transient stress periods are of variable length, but with the most recent years simulated with relatively short 6-month stress periods. The historical changes in the number of wells and total pumpage incorporated into the model are detailed by Clark and Hart (2009, fig. 10). Specific yield and specific storage values were estimated during the calibration process. Clark and Hart (2009) report that optimal values of specific yield range from 0.10 to 0.30 and for specific storage range from 8.5×10^{-7} m[-1] to 2.1×10^{-2} m[-1]. Additional information about hydraulic properties, boundary conditions, and the calibration process for the model are described in detail by Clark and Hart (2009).

The water budget computed by the model indicated that the total cumulative depletion in 2000 was 117.6 km[3] and in 2007 was 173.2 km[3] (fig. 17; table 1). The depletion in 2008 was extrapolated by assuming that the average rate calculated during the previous 3 years applied during 2008. This results in an estimate of 182.0 km[3] of depletion for 2008 (table 1).

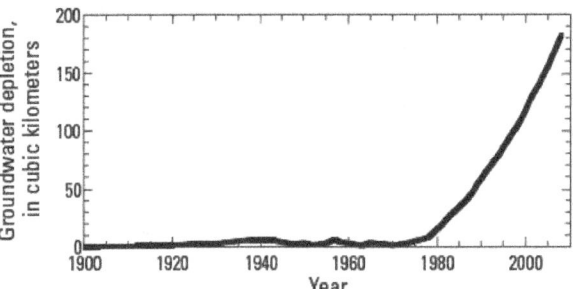

Figure 17.   Cumulative groundwater depletion in the Mississippi embayment, 1900 through 2008.

Gulf Coastal Plain: Total

The Gulf Coast regional aquifer systems comprise one of the largest, most complicated, and interdependent aquifer systems in the United States (Williamson and Grubb, 2001), encompassing an area of approximately 600,000 km[2]. A total of nearly 14 km[3]/yr was withdrawn from the aquifers in 1985. Depletion in the Gulf Coastal Plain was estimated in five separate subareas, as described above. Integrating these estimates yields a total cumulative depletion since 1900 of about 198.5 km[3] in 2000 and 266.0 km[3] in 2008 (table 1).

High Plains Aquifer

The High Plains (or Ogallala) aquifer underlies about 450,000 km² in the central United States (figs. 1 and 2) and represents the principal source of water for irrigation and drinking in this major agricultural area (Dennehy and others, 2002; McGuire and others, 2003). The High Plains aquifer is generally unconfined and composed of unconsolidated alluvial deposits. The hydrogeologic framework of the aquifer system is described by Weeks and others (1988). The 30-year average annual precipitation ranges from about 36 cm in the west to about 81 cm in the eastern part of the aquifer. Evaporation rates are high relative to precipitation, so there is little water available to recharge the aquifer (Dennehy and others, 2002). Potential recharge in non-irrigated areas has been estimated to range from less than 6 mm along the western boundary of the aquifer to as much as 127 mm in the northeastern part of the High Plains aquifer (Dennehy and others, 2002; Dugan and Zelt, 2000).

Substantial pumping of the High Plains aquifer for irrigation since the 1940s has resulted in large water-table declines (exceeding 50 m in places) and depletion of groundwater in storage in the system (Dennehy and others, 2002). The High Plains aquifer is one of the most extensively monitored aquifer systems in the United States, with the magnitude of depletion carefully assessed and documented (for example, McGuire, 2001, 2003, 2004). Annual pumpage from the High Plains aquifer for irrigation increased from 5 to 23 km³/yr from 1949 to 1974; annual pumpage did not change greatly from 1974 to 1995 (McGuire and others, 2003).

The use of groundwater from the High Plains aquifer resulted in substantial water-level declines (McGuire and others, 2003). By 1980, more than 30 m of water-level declines had occurred in some parts of the aquifer, and by 1999 withdrawals resulted in more than 12 m of additional water-level decline in larger areas (Luckey and others, 1981; McGuire, 2001).

Maps of water-level changes since predevelopment conditions (assumed to be prior to 1950) provide the primary basis for estimates of groundwater depletion (for example, fig. 18). The change in the volume of water in storage in the High Plains aquifer was calculated by using area-weighted, average specific yield of the aquifer (15.1 percent) and change in aquifer volume (McGuire, 2007).

Depletion estimates presented by McGuire (2004, 2007, 2009, 2011) are generally based on water-level measurements made during winter months early in a given year. It is assumed that these are representative of storage changes at the end of the previous calendar year. After this adjustment, McGuire's data indicate that the total cumulative groundwater depletion from 1950 through the end of 2000 is about 255 km³. By the end of 2008, the total depletion is about 337 km³ (McGuire, 2011, table 3). McGuire and others (2003) and McGuire (2009, 2011) also present a breakdown by State for the depletion estimates at specific times. The fraction of the total depletion attributable to the components in the various States

has varied with time, and sufficient data are not available to estimate how the rates of depletion in individual States varied with time during 1900–2000 (table 2).

Groundwater pumpage in the Texas and New Mexico part of the High Plains was substantial prior to 1950, with pumpage in Texas being about 10 times greater than in New Mexico (Gaum, 1953). In the Texas part of the High Plains aquifer, it is reported that water-table declines "of a foot or more were recorded throughout the 1940s" and that in 1949 pumpage for irrigation was about 4.9 km³/yr (High Plains Underground Water Conservation District No. 1, 2010). About 22.2 km³ of saturated materials were dewatered in the High Plains of Texas during 1938–49 (Gaum, 1953). Assuming that the average specific yield is about 16 percent, and that depletion in the High Plains of New Mexico was 10 percent of that in Texas, it is estimated that an additional 4.0 km³ of depletion occurred prior to 1950 and is not included in the published estimates of depletion from the High Plains aquifer. Insufficient data are available to estimate pre-1950 depletion in other parts of the High Plains.

Merging the estimates for Texas in the 1940s with the temporal calculations of McGuire (2009, 2011) since 1950 yields a plot showing the changes in groundwater storage over time (fig. 19). This plot indicates that the water levels and depletion in the High Plains aquifer have not yet stabilized, and since 2000 appear to be continuing at as high a rate as ever. The depletion during the last 8 years of record (2001–2008, inclusive) is about 32 percent of the cumulative depletion during the entire 20th century, and the rate of depletion during this recent period averaged about 10.2 km³/yr. The total depletion by the end of 2000 is about 259 km³ and by the end of 2008 is about 341 km³ (table 1). The estimated depletion for 2008 is revised slightly from the estimate of Konikow (2011) based on revised estimates by McGuire (2011) and revised estimates of pre-1950 depletion.

Central Valley, California

The Central Valley of California is a major agricultural area in a large valley with an area of about 52,000 km² (Williamson and others, 1989; Bertoldi and others, 1991) (figs. 1 and 2). The Central Valley includes the Sacramento Valley, the San Joaquin Valley, and the Tulare Basin. The Central Valley has an arid to semiarid Mediterranean climate, where the average annual precipitation ranges from 33 to 66 cm in the Sacramento Valley and from 13 to 41 cm in the San Joaquin Valley (Bertoldi and others, 1991). Streamflow is an important factor in the water supply of the valley. It is entirely dependent on precipitation in the Sierra Nevada to the east and in parts of the Klamath Mountains in the north (Williamson and others, 1989).

Geologically, the valley is a large asymmetric trough that is bounded by granitic, metamorphic, and marine sedimentary rocks. The trough is filled with a thick sequence (up to 16 km)

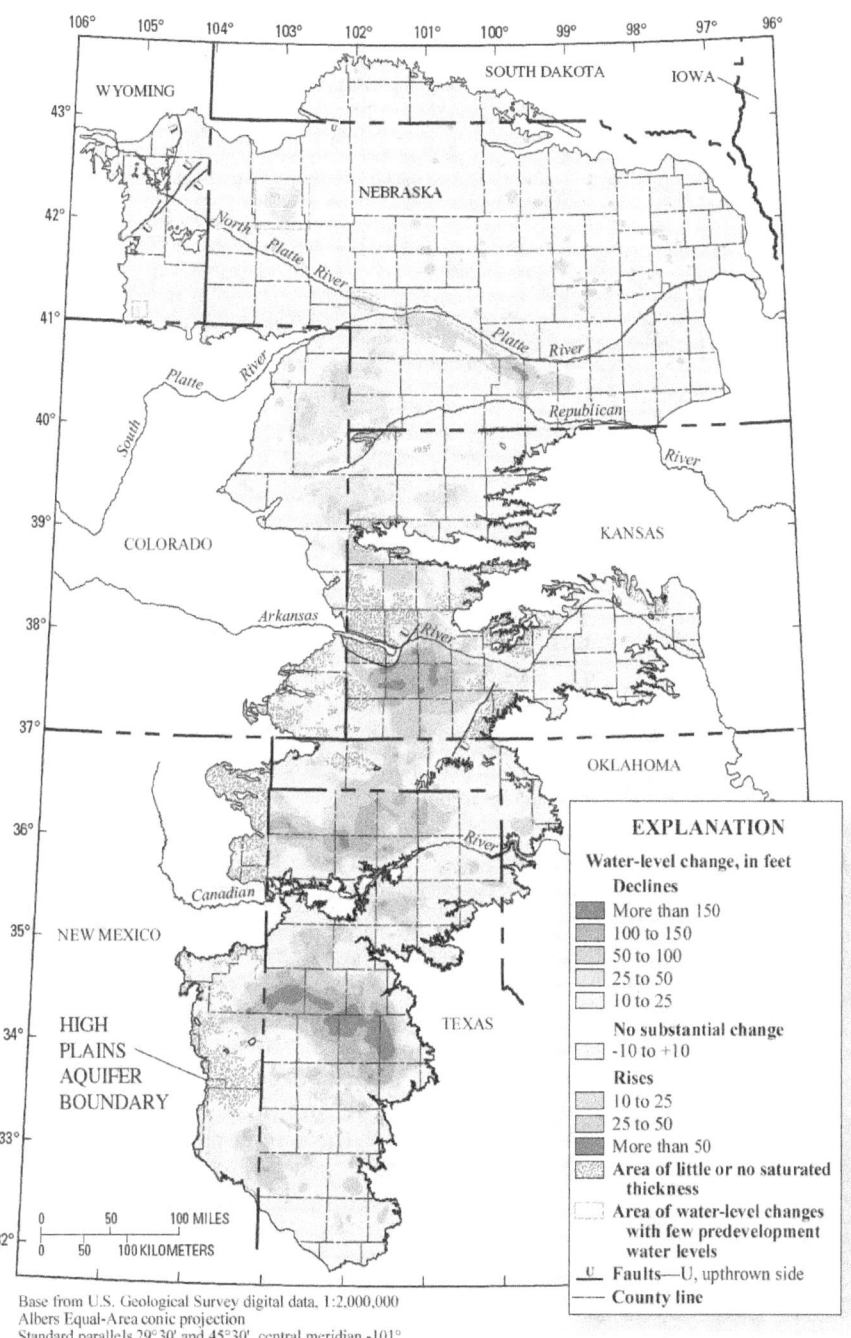

Figure 18. Water-level changes in the High Plains aquifer, predevelopment through 2007 (from McGuire, 2009, as modified from Lowry and others, 1967; Luckey and others, 1981; Gutentag and others, 1984; and Burbach, 2007).

of alluvial sediments. Page (1986) describes the geology of the area in more detail.

The aquifer system is composed of interlayered gravel, sand, silt, and clay derived from the surrounding mountains (Bertoldi, 1989). The thickness of sediments comprising the freshwater parts of the aquifer averages about 880 m in the San Joaquin Valley and 460 m in the Sacramento Valley. The shallow part of the aquifer system is unconfined, whereas the deeper part is semiconfined or confined (Bertoldi, 1989).

Groundwater development began in the Central Valley around 1880. By 1913, total well pumpage for the

Central Valley was about 0.44 km^3 annually (Bertoldi and others, 1991). During the 1940s and 1950s, the pumpage increased sharply, and by the 1960s and 1970s averaged about 14.2 km^3/yr. By the 1980s there were approximately 100,000 high-capacity wells in the Central Valley for either irrigation or municipal supply.

In the late 1960s, increased importation of surface water caused groundwater pumpage to decline (Bertoldi and others, 1991). However, a drought during 1976–77 decreased the availability of surface water, and groundwater pumpage increased to a maximum of 18.5 km^3 in 1977. During

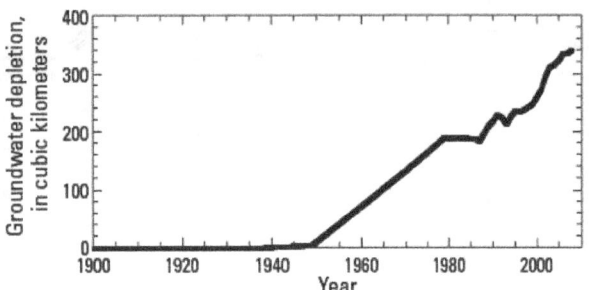

Figure 19. Cumulative groundwater depletion in the High Plains aquifer, 1900 through 2008.

1962–2003, the average withdrawals from irrigation wells was estimated to have averaged about 10.6 km³/yr (Faunt and others, 2009a).

Heavy groundwater use in parts of the Central Valley has caused continuous water-level declines (Bertoldi, 1989). In parts of the San Joaquin Valley and Tulare Basin, water levels had declined nearly 122 m, depleting groundwater from storage and lowering water levels to as much as 30 m below sea level. Long-term water-level records in some wells (fig. 20) indicate that water levels were already declining at substantial rates when water levels were first observed as early as the 1930s (Williamson and others, 1989). The extensive groundwater pumping caused changes to the groundwater flow system, changes in water levels, changes in aquifer storage, and widespread land subsidence in the San Joaquin Valley, which began in the 1920s (Ireland and others, 1984; Bertoldi and others, 1991).

A 3D, transient, groundwater-flow model was developed to help analyze the aquifer system (Williamson and others, 1989). The model area was discretized into a uniformly spaced grid consisting of square cells measuring 9.65 km on a side. Vertically the model used four layers. The model was calibrated for both steady-state predevelopment conditions and transient postdevelopment conditions for 1961–77. An updated and refined transient groundwater-flow model was developed for 1961–2003 (Faunt and others, 2009b). The new model

used MODFLOW-2000 (Harbaugh and others, 2000) with the Farm Process (Schmid and others, 2006). The refined grid included 441 rows, 98 columns, and 10 layers. The uniform grid spacing was 1.61 km on a side; model layers generally thicken with depth (Faunt and others, 2009b).

The total decrease in groundwater storage from predevelopment conditions until 1961 was estimated to be about 58 km³ (Williamson and others, 1989, p. 95). The updated model (Faunt and others, 2009b) indicates that the decrease in groundwater storage from 1961 through 2000 was about 55.4 km³, and that the depletion further increased to about 71.2 km³ by 2003. The total depletion in the Central Valley during the 20th century is thus estimated to equal 113 km³. About 20 percent of this depletion is related to land subsidence.

By assuming that the depletion is related strongly to groundwater extraction rates and average rates of water-level declines, an approximate curve showing the transient changes in storage can be constructed. Pumpage in the San Joaquin Valley increased almost linearly from about 1900 through 1945, and grew at notably faster rates after that (Galloway and others, 1999). Plots of subsidence versus time indicate little to no subsidence prior to about 1925 (Galloway and others, 1999). Well hydrographs for the period of 1900–60 generally do not show data prior to 1925 (Williamson and others, 1989), so it is assumed that there was no significant depletion prior to then. Declines generally proceed linearly at a relatively slower rate during 1925–45, and a faster rate during 1946–60. In order to estimate the rates of depletion and cumulative depletion over time, a simplifying assumption is made that approximately 25 percent of the water-level decline and related depletion occurred during the earlier period, and 75 percent during the latter period.

The model results include the simulated annual changes in aquifer-system storage for 1962–2003 (Faunt and others, 2009a, fig. B9). During the final two years of this period, the average rate of depletion was 4.27 km³/yr. Data from the GRACE satellite were used to estimate groundwater depletion in the Central Valley for a 78-month period from October 2003 through March 2010 (Famiglietti and others, 2011). The average

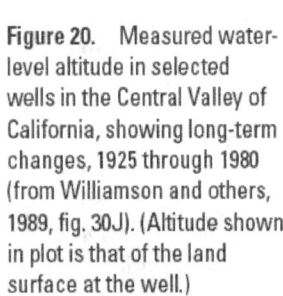

Figure 20. Measured water-level altitude in selected wells in the Central Valley of California, showing long-term changes, 1925 through 1980 (from Williamson and others, 1989, fig. 30J). (Altitude shown in plot is that of the land surface at the well.)

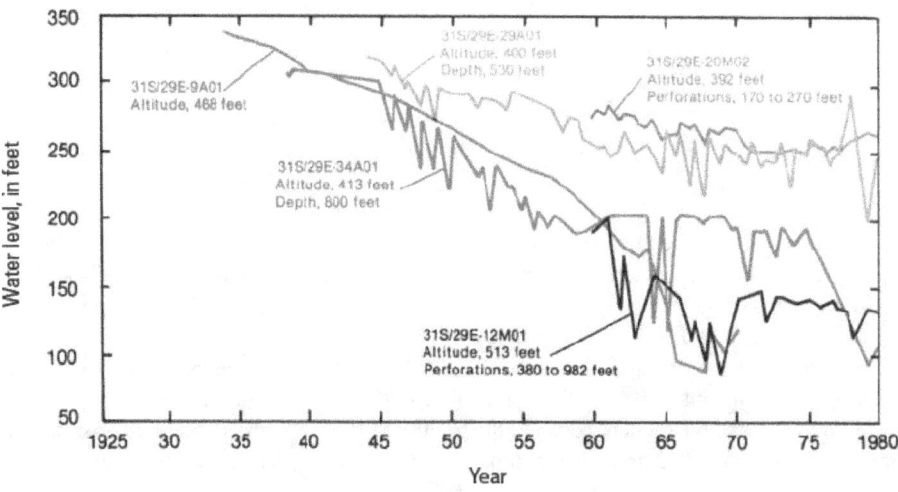

rate of depletion during this period was 0.26 km³/month (3.12 km³/yr), which is similar to the rate computed by the model during 2002–03. Assuming that the rate computed from satellite gravity data applies from 2004 through 2008, this results in a total cumulative net groundwater depletion at the end of 2008 of about 145 km³ (fig. 21; table 1).

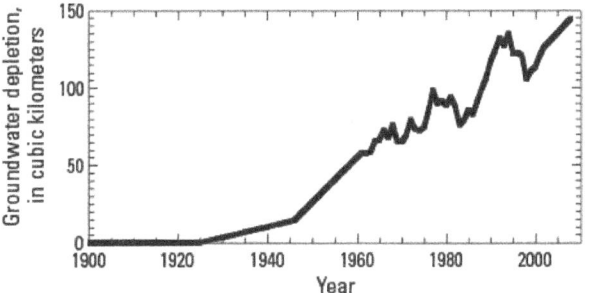

Figure 21. Cumulative groundwater depletion in the Central Valley of California, 1900 through 2008.

Western Alluvial Basins

Alluvial Basins, Arizona

The Southwest alluvial basins include an area of 212,000 km² in south-central Arizona and small parts of adjacent States (figs. 1 and 2). The area includes 72 separately identifiable basins (Anderson and others, 1992). The basins are filled with unconsolidated alluvial deposits that are as much as 3,000 m thick (Anderson, 1995). The hydrogeology and water resources are discussed in more detail by Anderson and others (1992). The area has an arid to semiarid climate, and the precipitation generally ranges from 8 to 76 cm (Anderson and others, 1992).

Development of water resources was principally for agriculture and was started in the 1860s (Anderson and others, 1992). Groundwater withdrawals began in the late 1800s, and by 1942, groundwater pumpage totaled 2.1 km³/yr. Rapid agricultural growth followed, and by 1952, groundwater pumpage was 4.7 km³/yr. During 1950–80, groundwater pumpage averaged more than 5.9 km³/yr. The withdrawals greatly exceeded recharge, so large water-level declines resulted, generally in the range of 15 to 140 m, but more than 180 m in places (Galloway and others, 1999). This also resulted in land subsidence. By 1980, a total of 227 km³ of groundwater had been withdrawn. More than 50 percent of this volume (113.5 km³) was removed from aquifer storage (Anderson and others, 1992).

Annual groundwater pumpage is documented for 1915 through 1990 (Leake and others, 2000). To reconstruct a time history of cumulative depletion, it is assumed that the rate of growth of depletion during 1915–80 parallels the annual pumpage data. On this basis, about half the total cumulative

pumpage and half the cumulative depletion would have occurred in 1961.

With the recognition of serious problems of subsidence and water-table declines, water management and water-use patterns and practices changed after 1980. Also, the construction of an aqueduct to import surface water from the Colorado River since 1985 led to decreases in groundwater withdrawals and implementation of artificial recharge programs (Galloway and others, 1999). These measures have resulted in cessation of water-level declines in many areas and the recovery of water levels in some areas, although compaction and subsidence persist in some basins (Galloway and others, 1999).

Tillman and Leake (2010) analyzed trends in groundwater levels in the area for 1970–2008. Their database included more than 127,000 records from hundreds of wells in five Active Management Areas (AMA) (Tillman and Leake, 2010). The analysis indicated that the number of wells with rising water-level trends increased and the number of wells with falling trends decreased during 1980–95, but those trends in water levels were reversed during the 1995–2004 time period (Tillman and Leake, 2010). However, the general trends were not always consistent among the five basins. For example, during 2000–2008, more than half the wells (66 percent) in the Prescott, Santa Cruz, and Tucson areas showed falling water levels, but only 32 percent of the wells in the Phoenix and Pinal areas showed falling water levels. The annual water demand satisfied by well pumpage during 1980–2008 has increased slightly in the Santa Cruz, Tucson, and Prescott areas, and has more noticeably decreased in the Phoenix and Pinal areas (Tillman and Leake, 2010, fig. 5). On the whole, the net decrease in pumpage for the entire area averaged about 0.045 km³/yr.

A transient, 3D, groundwater-flow model of the Salt River Valley part of the Phoenix AMA was developed and calibrated by Freihoefer and others (2009) using MODFLOW-2000 (Harbaugh and others, 2000). The Salt River Valley area encompasses almost half of the area of the Phoenix AMA. The model included 3 layers, 125 rows, and 222 columns using square cells that were 0.80 km on a side. The model stresses included a representation of increased recharge—primarily from artificial recharge programs. Additional descriptions of hydraulic properties, boundary conditions, and the calibration process are provided by Freihoefer and others (2009). The model results indicated a net increase in the volume of groundwater in storage of about 4.92 km³ during the 24-year simulation period, or an average rate of 0.205 km³/yr.

Assuming that rate of change in storage in the Salt River Valley is representative of the rest of the Phoenix AMA, and that this represents the bulk of the storage change in all of the Arizona alluvial basins, the change in storage during 1981–2008 can be estimated by assuming an average linear trend of 0.41 km³/yr added to storage in the alluvial basins of Arizona during 1981–2008. On this basis, the total cumulative groundwater depletion in 2000 was 105.3 km³ and in 2008 was 102.0 km³ (fig. 22; table 1). This compares favorably with the recent estimate by Tillman and others (2011) that the total storage change (depletion) through 1987 was 91.9 km³. Tillman and others (2011) specifically note that their total storage change is probably underestimated because they only analyzed 15 basins that accounted for 85 percent of the total historical withdrawals and because their estimates do not include loss of storage from land subsidence.

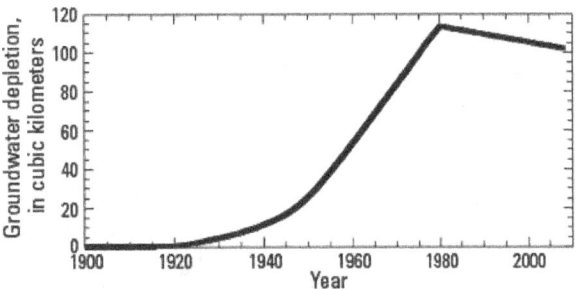

Figure 22. Cumulative groundwater depletion in the alluvial basins of Arizona, 1900 through 2008.

Antelope Valley, California

Antelope Valley is a topographically closed basin in the western part of the Mojave Desert in southern California (Leighton and Phillips, 2003) (figs. 1 and 2). The climate is semiarid to arid, and the average annual precipitation in the interior of the valley is less than 25 cm. The Antelope Valley groundwater basin includes an area of about 2,400 km². Prior to 1972, groundwater provided more than 90 percent of the total water supply in the valley; since 1972, it has provided between 50 and 90 percent. Pumpage peaked at more than 0.37 km³/yr in the 1950s and 60s, and by the mid-1980s had declined to about 0.12 km³/yr (Galloway and others, 2003). More details of historical groundwater use are documented by Templin and others (1995) and Leighton and Phillips (2003). Groundwater-level declines of more than 60 m in some parts of the groundwater basin have resulted in an increase in pumping lifts, reduced well efficiency, and land subsidence of more than 2 m in some areas (Ikehara and Phillips, 1994; Leighton and Phillips, 2003). Subsidence during 1930–92 caused a storage loss of more than 0.06 km³ (Ikehara and Phillips, 1994).

The groundwater flow system consists of three aquifers: the upper, middle, and lower aquifers (Leighton and Phillips, 2003). The aquifer system consist of unconsolidated deposits of gravel, sand, silt, and clay alluvial deposits and clay and silty clay lacustrine deposits. The basin-fill deposits are more than 1,500 m thick in places.

A 3D transient model was developed and calibrated to simulate groundwater flow and aquifer-system compaction in the area (Leighton and Phillips, 2003). The model used the MODFLOW code (McDonald and Harbaugh, 1988). The model grid consists of 43 rows and 60 columns forming 2,580 square cells with a length of 1,609 m on a side. The

aquifer system was discretized vertically into three layers. The model was first calibrated for steady-state flow to represent predevelopment conditions prior to 1915. Then the transient model was developed using 81 one-year stress periods to simulate the period of 1915–1995 inclusive. More detailed descriptions of model parameters, boundary conditions, and the calibration process are presented by Leighton and Phillips (2003).

The results of the transient simulation indicate that more than 10.5 km³ of groundwater was removed from storage during 1915–95, with most of the storage change occurring between about 1945 and 1975 (Leighton and Phillips, 2003). Groundwater storage changed little during the final 10 years of the simulation period because discharge by pumpage had declined sufficiently to be balanced by recharge. During the final 10 years of the simulation, the average rate of depletion was 0.005 km³/yr. That low rate was used to extrapolate the cumulative depletion through 2008. This indicates that the total cumulative depletion in 2000 is about 10.5 km³ and in 2008 is about 10.6 km³ (fig. 23; table 1).

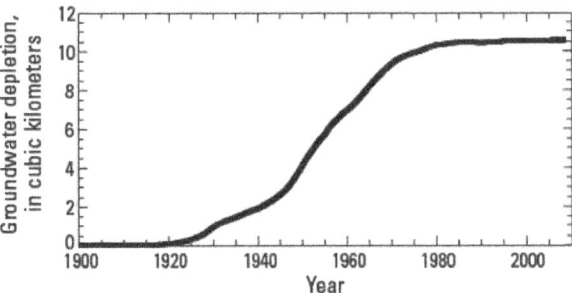

Figure 23. Cumulative groundwater depletion in Antelope Valley, California, 1900 through 2008.

Coachella Valley, California

The Coachella Valley is a 100-km long, northwest-trending valley in southern California that includes an area of about 1,000 km² (Sneed and others, 2002) (figs. 1 and 2). It has an arid climate, with an average annual rainfall as low as 8 cm on the valley floor. Sneed and others (2002) report that the valley is filled with as much as 3,700 m of sediments. The water-bearing deposits lie within the upper 610 m of the system and consist of "a complex unconsolidated to partly consolidated assemblage of gravel, sand, silt, and clay of alluvial and lacustrine origins" (Sneed and others, 2002, p. 5). More information on the hydrogeology and groundwater use in the area is presented by Reichard and Meadows (1992).

Since the early 1920s, groundwater has been a major source of agricultural, municipal, and domestic supply in the valley (Sneed and others, 2002). Pumping of groundwater resulted in water-level declines as large as 15 m through the late 1940s. In 1949, the importation of Colorado River water to the lower Coachella Valley began, resulting in a reduction in groundwater pumping and a recovery of water levels during the 1950s through the 1970s. Since the late 1970s, demand for water in the valley has exceeded deliveries of imported surface water, resulting in increased pumping and associated groundwater-level declines and subsidence. Numerous well hydrographs indicate steady continuing declines in water levels from the 1980s through 2000, although there were a few wells showing recovery during 1995–2000 (Sneed and others, 2002). In 2000, some water levels were at the lowest levels in their recorded histories (Sneed and others, 2002). More recent measurements during 2003–2009 indicate that subsidence has increased by a factor of two since 2003 in several urban areas within the valley, and that water levels in most wells in these areas continued to decline to their lowest recorded levels (Sneed, 2010).

An electric-analog model of groundwater flow was developed for the upper Coachella Valley (Tyley, 1974). Based on an analysis of observed water-level changes and spatial variations in specific yield, the total decrease in groundwater storage during 1953–67 was estimated at about 0.74 km^3 (Tyley, 1974). Specific yield ranged from 0.06 to 0.18, with an areally weighted average of about 0.15 (Tyley, 1974, fig. 5).

A finite-element model was developed and calibrated by Swain (1978) for the upper Coachella Valley—the part of the valley where most of the decline occurs. An initial steady-state model was developed to simulate predevelopment conditions prior to 1936, and a transient simulation model was applied for the period 1936–74. Calibration was based in part on a map of observed water-level declines during 1936–73 (Swain, 1978, fig. 4). The calibrated model was then used to predict the effects of artificial recharge (Swain, 1978). Integrating the observed water-level changes over the study area and multiplying by an average specific yield of 0.15 indicates that the total depletion during 1936–73 was about 1.2 km^3.

The model and its predictions were subsequently evaluated and the model simulation period extended through 1986 using a newer updated finite-element model (Reichard and Meadows, 1992). The calculated water budgets from these two models were not published in detail, so no information is readily available on computed changes in storage by the models. However, the net pumpage (defined as the quantity of water actually removed from the groundwater system) is about 65 percent of the gross pumpage (Reichard and Meadows, 1992). The reported net pumpage of Reichard and Meadows (1992) during 1953–67 equals about 0.744 km^3, which matches the earlier depletion estimate of Tyley (1974), which was based on measured changes in water levels, with less than 1 percent difference. The reported net pumpage of Reichard and Meadows (1992) during 1936–73 equals about 1.37 km^3, which is about 14 percent higher than the depletion estimate based on water-level changes shown by Swain (1978). Based on these two comparisons, it is assumed that for the longer simulation period (1936–86) of the updated model (Reichard and Meadows, 1992), depletion is approximately equal to 86 percent of the net pumpage. On this basis, the total depletion during 1936–86 is about 2.33 km^3.

The average rate of depletion during the final four years of that period is approximately 0.12 km^3/yr. Most observation wells indicate a general continuation of the water-level declines from the 1980s through 2008—a trend that provides a basis for extrapolating beyond 1986. Conservatively, it is assumed that depletion continued through 2008 at half the rate estimated for 1983–86. A plot of the estimated change in groundwater depletion during 1900–2008 is shown in figure 24. This estimate indicates that the total cumulative depletion in 2000 is about 3.2 km^3 and in 2008 is about 3.7 km^3 (table 1).

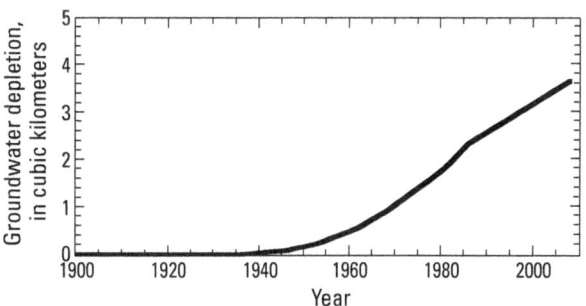

Figure 24. Cumulative groundwater depletion in the Coachella Valley, California, 1900 through 2008.

Death Valley Region, California and Nevada

The Death Valley Regional Flow System (DVRFS) encompasses approximately 100,000 km^2 of southern Nevada and southeastern California (figs. 1 and 2). The aquifer system is composed of carbonate, volcanic, and alluvial rock units. Development of groundwater resources began in the early 1900s to supply local, large-scale agriculture, and development grew to support increased domestic, mining, industry, and livestock supply demands (Belcher and others, 2010).

The DVRFS includes several prominent valleys, including Death Valley, Amargosa Desert, and Pahrump Valley. Mountain ranges occupy about 25 percent of the land surface, and the remainder is occupied by broad intermontane basins. The basins are filled with sediment and some interbedded volcanic deposits. Within the basins, another 10 percent of the study area contains evaporation playas and alluvial flats (Belcher and others, 2010).

The area has a desert climate. Surface waters are limited in the region and are predominantly supported by regional groundwater discharge. Several spring pools and manmade reservoirs are located in the Amargosa Desert (Belcher and others, 2010).

The DVRFS study area is located within the southern Great Basin, a subprovince of the Basin and Range physiographic province. The subsurface geology of the region is very complex and variable because of a long and changing tectonic history. A more detailed description of the geology in the region is given by Belcher and others (2002) and Sweetkind and others (2010).

Hydrogeologic units forming the framework of the groundwater flow system are defined on the basis of rocks and deposits that have considerable lateral extent and relatively distinct hydrogeologic properties. The major units of the groundwater flow system, from oldest to youngest, are the lower clastic confining unit, the lower carbonate aquifer, the upper clastic confining unit, the upper carbonate aquifer, the volcanic aquifers and confining units, and the alluvial aquifer (Belcher and others, 2002). The most extensive and transmissive aquifer in the region is the lower carbonate aquifer. The alluvial aquifers are an important, but a discontinuous, groundwater resource in the region (Belcher and others, 2002).

Most natural recharge in the region results from infiltration of precipitation and runoff and as inflow from adjacent carbonate aquifers. Deep infiltration occurs along streams flowing through basin fill deposits and as snowmelt on volcanic or carbonate rock outcrops (Faunt and others, 2010a).

Natural discharge in the region is by evapotranspiration and by outflow from springs and across regional boundaries. Most of the groundwater discharge is consumed by evapotranspiration where the water table is near the surface or at spring locations. Local natural discharge areas, typified as dry playas, wetlands, or a combination of the two, represent less than 5 percent of the total model area.

Groundwater pumpage within the study area began around 1913 in Pahrump Valley. Pumpage began mainly to support rising agricultural interests, but also supplied mining, industry, rural, and urban growth. The number of pumping wells in the region had increased from three in 1913 to over 9,300 in 1998. Pumpage for irrigation in the DVRFS accounted for nearly 91 percent of total groundwater withdrawals through the year 1998. Annual pumpage estimates by

San Juan and others (2010) for 1913–1998 (fig. 25) show that annual withdrawals increased from 4.9 million m³ in 1913 to 93.8 million m³ in 1998, with a substantial increase in pumpage rates after 1945. In total, 3.2 km³ of groundwater was withdrawn from the study area from 1913 to 1998 (San Juan and others, 2010).

A three-dimensional groundwater-flow model of the DVRFS was developed by Faunt and others (2010b) using MODFLOW-2000 (Harbaugh and others, 2000). A steady-state model was first calibrated for the predevelopment hydrologic conditions of water year 1913. A transient model was developed next to represent long-term water-level changes from the predevelopment time (1913) to 1998. Each year of the 86-year transient simulation was divided into two stress periods.

The flow model covers an area of approximately 82,000 km², and the grid resolution is 1,500 m. In total, the finite-difference grid consisted of 194 rows and 160 columns. Vertically, the hydrogeologic units were represented in 16 model layers with thicknesses ranging from 50 to more than 300 m (Faunt and others, 2010b).

The groundwater-flow model was calibrated to hydraulic-head and groundwater-discharge observations. Other hydraulic conditions, boundary properties, and calibration methods are described in more detail by Faunt and others (2010b).

The model-computed water budget for the transient simulation showed that a net volume of 3.2 km³ of groundwater was removed from storage in the DVRFS during 1913–98. The average rate of depletion during the last 10 years of the simulation was about 0.0797 km³/yr. Extrapolation of this rate through 2008 indicates that the total net depletion in 2000 is about 3.4 km³ and in 2008 is about 4.0 km³ (fig. 26; table 1).

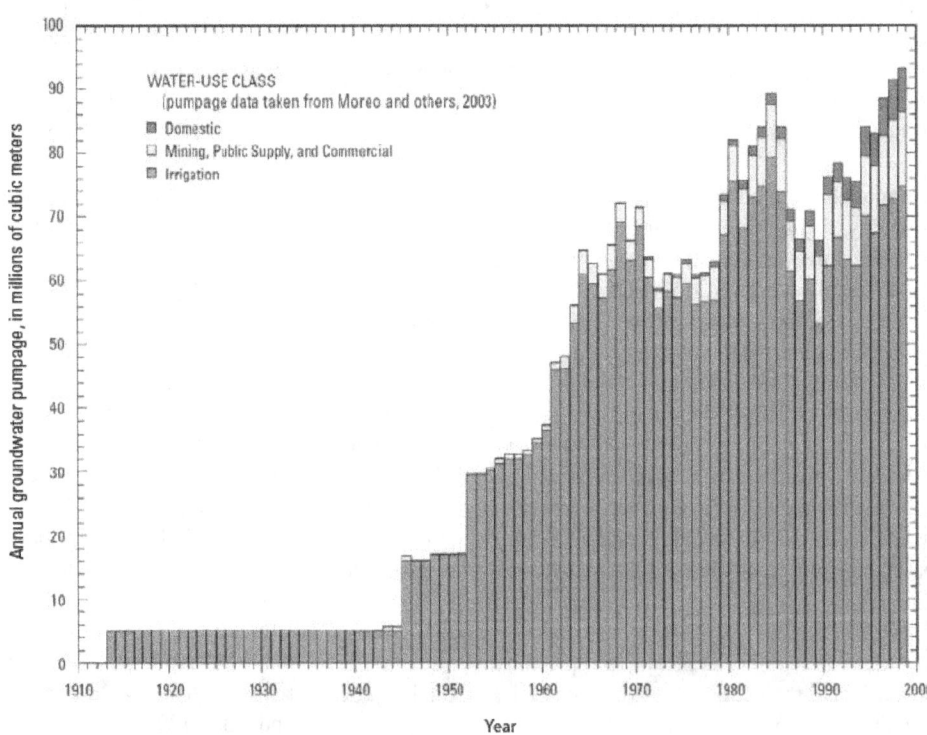

Figure 25. Annual groundwater withdrawal estimates by water-use class from the Death Valley regional flow system, 1913 through 1998 (San Juan and others, 2010, fig. C-5).

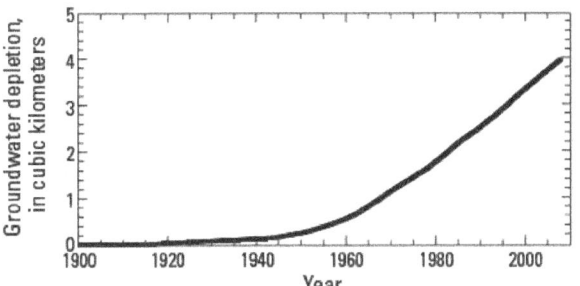

Figure 26. Cumulative groundwater depletion in the Death Valley regional flow system, California, 1900 through 2008.

Escalante Valley, Utah

The Beryl-Enterprise area of the Escalante Desert in the Basin and Range physiographic province covers an area of about 4,970 km² in southwestern Utah (figs. 1 and 2). The aquifer system in this area consists of saturated unconsolidated to semi-consolidated valley fill. Large declines in water-table levels resulted from groundwater development in the region (Mower, 1982).

The central part of the area is a desert valley. The average annual precipitation (1931–60) is less than 30.5 cm in most of the irrigated parts of the area and ranges from about 2 to 76 cm in the mountains. Average yearly pan evaporation in the nearby Milford area during April through October (1953–78) was 198 cm. The hydrology of the Beryl-Enterprise area of the Escalante Desert is described in detail by Mower (1982).

Unconsolidated to semi-consolidated gravel, sand, silt, and clay forms most of the principal aquifer. Thickness ranges from zero near the edge of the valley to more than 300 m in the central part of the valley. Locally, discontinuous clay and silt deposits impede vertical flow but do not prevent vertical movement of groundwater between the coarser deposits.

Recharge into the area comes partly by infiltration from losing stream channels, irrigation, and precipitation on the valley floor. With improved irrigation systems installed by 1977, irrigation efficiency increased and the irrigation losses to these factors decreased to about 20 percent. Direct infiltration on the valley floor from precipitation is negligible, except when already saturated irrigated land allows downward movement of the precipitation (Mower, 1982). Another significant source of recharge to the area occurs through lateral subsurface inflow.

A small percentage of the groundwater discharge occurs by evapotranspiration and subsurface outflow. A majority of the discharge from the Beryl-Enterprise area comes from public, industrial, and agricultural well withdrawals. Wells in the area were first drilled into the area for domestic and stock supply in the late 19th century and early 20th century. The first irrigation well was constructed in 1919, and withdrawals averaged about 0.003 km³/yr until 1936. Estimates of total annual groundwater withdrawals from 1937 through 2000 (fig. 27) indicate that annual withdrawals remained small and fairly constant until 1945, when they sharply increased to 0.11 km³/yr by 1974 (Christiansen, 2002). Improved irrigation systems after 1974 reduced the amount of groundwater withdrawals in the region (Mower, 1982). From the late 1980s to 2000, withdrawals averaged approximately 0.10 km³/yr (Christiansen, 2002). A general decline in water levels has been observed throughout the valley since the 1950s (Christiansen, 2002). One representative well to the northeast of the Beryl Junction area showed declines of about 29 m (fig. 28); some other wells show even greater declines (Christiansen, 2002, fig. 31).

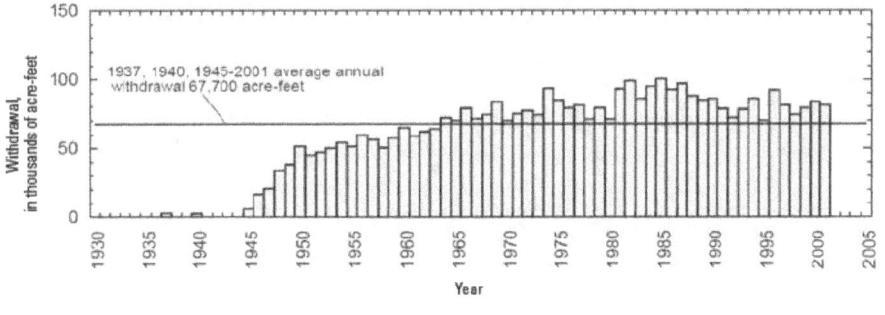

Figure 27. Annual withdrawals from wells in the Beryl-Enterprise area of Utah (from Christiansen, 2002, fig. 31). Long-term average withdrawal rate is about 0.08 km³/yr.

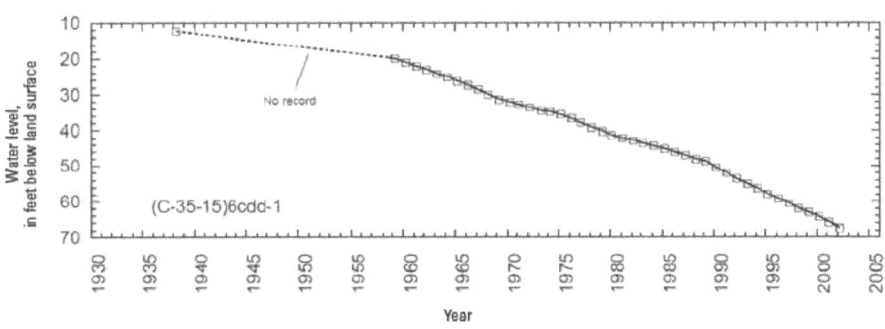

Figure 28. Long-term changes in water levels in a well in the Beryl-Enterprise area of Utah (from Christiansen, 2002, fig. 31).

A two-dimensional groundwater-flow model for the Beryl-Enterprise area of the Escalante Valley was developed (Mower, 1982) using the model of Trescott and others (1976). The transient simulation represents the years from 1937 to 1977, and the simulation period is divided into five stress periods of irregular duration. The model used a variably spaced rectangular grid in which grid dimensions varied from 610 m in areas of relatively intense groundwater development to 4,570 m in areas with little or no groundwater development.

Specific yield values from long-term aquifer tests ranged from 0.04 to 0.20. Model calibration resulted in modeled specific yield values that varied from 0.20 for coarse valley fill deposits to 0.10 in areas of greatest water-level declines and only partial drainage (Mower, 1982, p. 48).

Using the values of specific yield from the groundwater model and measured water-level declines for the simulation period, a decrease in storage was estimated for the years 1937 to 1977 (Mower, 1982). The total groundwater depletion was 1.6 km^3.

Groundwater development continued after 1977 at about the same rate as during the last 10 years of the model simulation period. Groundwater levels also continued to decline at about the same rate as observed during the latter part of the pre-1977 period. On this basis, it is assumed that the ratio of groundwater depletion to groundwater withdrawal that was observed during the model simulation period (1937–77) would remain unchanged for the 1978–2000 period. Because the withdrawals during 1978–2000 (2.42 km^3) are almost equal to the withdrawals during 1937–77 (2.48 km^3), the estimated depletion during 1978–2000 was 1.6 km^3, equal to the estimated depletion for the 1937–77 period. Thus, the estimated total depletion in the Beryl-Enterprise area of the Escalante Valley, Utah, is about 3.2 km^3 for the period from 1937 to 2000 (table 1). The time rate of depletion (fig. 29) is assumed to be proportional to the fractional rate of cumulative withdrawals through 2000. During 1997–2000, withdrawals decreased, and the average rate of depletion was 0.065 km^3/yr. Assuming that this lower rate applies during 2001–2008, the rate yields a total groundwater depletion from storage for 1900 through 2008 of about 3.7 km^3 (table 1).

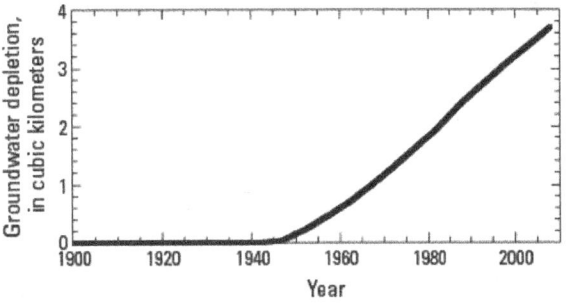

Figure 29.   Cumulative groundwater depletion in the Beryl-Enterprise area of the Escalante Valley, Utah, 1900 through 2008.

Estancia Basin, New Mexico

The Estancia Basin is a topographically closed basin in central New Mexico that has an area of about 6,200 km^2 (Shafike and Flanigan, 1999) (figs. 1 and 2). The climate is semiarid, and annual precipitation ranges from 28 to 58 cm (Shafike and Flanigan, 1999). The hydrology is described in more detail by Menking and others (2003). Groundwater is developed primarily from the valley-fill deposits. Substantial withdrawals began in the early 1940s—mostly to meet the demands of irrigated agriculture. The hydrogeology of the area is described in more detail by Shafike and Flanigan (1999).

A 3D transient MODFLOW model of the basin was developed and calibrated for the period 1940–96 (Shafike and Flanigan, 1999). The model-computed water budget indicated a total water depletion of about 2.6 km^3. Of this total, about 63 percent (1.6 km^3) was derived from a reduction of groundwater in storage (Shafike and Flanigan, 1999). A water-budget model developed for the basin indicates a decrease of groundwater in storage from 1910 to 1995 of about 1.9 km^3 (Thomas, 2004), which is in very close agreement with the model results (Shafike and Flanigan, 1999).

Based on the model analysis, 51 percent of the water depletions in 1996 are attributable to reductions of groundwater in storage (Shafike and Flanigan, 1999). Using data on groundwater pumpage and net depletion (consumptive use) (Shafike and Flanigan, 1999), assuming there is no depletion prior to 1940, and assuming that the reduction in groundwater storage is 63 percent of total reported water depletions for 1940–95 and 51 percent for 1996–2008, the time rate of depletion can be estimated (fig. 30). These results indicate that the cumulative net depletion of groundwater from storage was 1.7 km^3 for 1900 through 2000 and 1.9 km^3 for 1900 through 2008 (table 1).

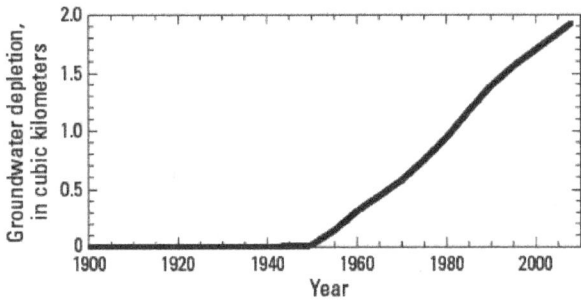

Figure 30.   Cumulative groundwater depletion in the Estancia Basin, New Mexico, 1900 through 2008.

Hueco Bolson, New Mexico and Texas

The Hueco Bolson is a sedimentary basin, roughly 320 km long and 40 km wide, that extends from New Mexico to the El Paso-Ciudad Juarez area of Texas and Mexico (figs. 1 and 2). The aquifer system has been a primary source of water for the area. With increased development and low recharge, large water-level declines, land subsidence, and water quality degradation have been observed.

Hueco Bolson has an arid continental climate. The mean annual precipitation is 20 cm in the El Paso area. Average annual pan evaporation near El Paso was 236 cm for 1985 to 1992 (Abeyta and Thomas, 1996). The Hueco Bolson partly drains into the Rio Grande (Abeyta and Thomas, 1996). Recharge occurs by mountain-front recharge, by seepage from the Rio Grande and from agricultural irrigation water, and from deep-well injection practices (Sheng and others, 2001).

The aquifer is in a structural depression bounded by faults associated with the Rio Grande Rift. Unconsolidated to poorly consolidated deposits of Tertiary and Quaternary age, consisting primarily of gravel, sand, silt, and clay, have filled the basin. Heywood and Yager (2003) provide a detailed description of the hydrogeology of the Hueco Bolson.

The first groundwater development in the El Paso region began in 1892. Thirty municipal wells were drilled but soon abandoned because of water-quality problems, leaving only one well functioning until 1904. By 1917, 44 wells were in the El Paso area, and from 1918 to 1943, the water supply for El Paso was pumped from two well fields. Water from the Rio Grande began to be utilized as a supplement to groundwater in 1943 (Groschen, 1994).

Recharge from river-derived irrigation led to a significant rise in groundwater levels. Agricultural drains were installed to control both the groundwater levels and soil salinization beginning in the 1930s. Many of the drains, however, were destroyed or not maintained since the early 1960s with development in the region (Heywood and Yager, 2003).

From 1940 to 1950, wells were drilled beneath the river alluvium, and by 1960, 107 large-capacity wells existed in El Paso. Ciudad Juarez, Mexico, across the Rio Grande from El Paso, had 33 municipal wells by 1963 (Groschen, 1994). With the extensive pumping during this time, two large cones

of depression had been detected under the two cities. By 1984, water levels had declined almost 46 m under El Paso. Annual groundwater withdrawals from the Hueco Bolson from 1903 to 1996 (fig. 31) show that pumpage reached its maximum in El Paso by the late 1980s at more than 0.23 km^3/yr (Heywood and Yager, 2003).

A 3D groundwater-flow model for the Hueco Bolson was developed by Heywood and Yager (2003) using MODFLOW-96 (Harbaugh and McDonald, 1996). The transient simulation represents the years from 1903 through 2002. The 1903 to 1996 period (inclusive) was simulated using annual stress periods, and the 1969 to 2002 period (inclusive) was simulated using monthly stress periods, so that there was an overlap of 28 years between the two versions of the model. The model included 10 layers, 165 rows, and 100 columns of cells with lengths 500 or 1,000 m on either side. The specific storage for the model was estimated to be 7×10^{-6} m^{-1}, and the specific yield was estimated to range from 0.10 to 0.20. Other hydraulic conditions, boundary properties, and calibration methods are described in detail by Heywood and Yager (2003).

The calibrated model computed an annual water budget for the aquifer system over the 100-years of simulation, including changes in storage (Heywood and Yager, 2003). The total groundwater depletion in the Hueco Bolson aquifer system (including the effects of interbed compaction) computed by the model for 1903–96 is 4.2 km^3, and the calculated depletion through the end of 2002 is 5.0 km^3.

The storage changes with time from the two versions of the model were used as the basis for computing a composite curve of groundwater depletion from storage during the period 1900–2008. The depletion from the annual model was extended from 1996 through 2002 using the rates of depletion for that period calculated with the model using monthly stress periods. Finally, the depletion values were extrapolated from 2003 through 2008 by assuming that the calculated rate

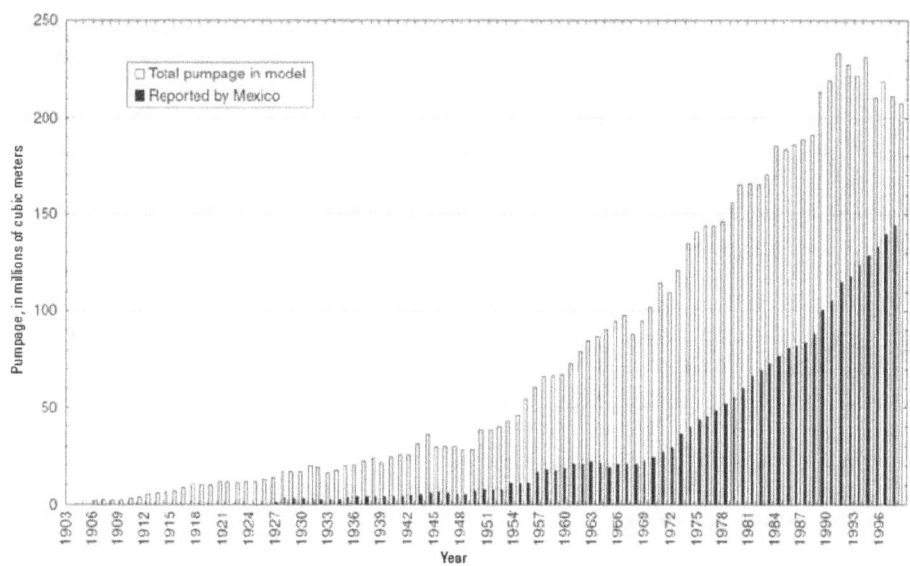

Figure 31. Groundwater withdrawals from the Hueco Bolson, 1903 through 1996 (from Heywood and Yager, 2003).

with the monthly model during its final 2 years of simulation (2001–02) also applied to 2003 through 2008. On this basis, the total groundwater depletion from storage during the 20th century was 4.6 km³ and by 2008 had increased to approximately 5.7 km³ (fig. 32; table 1).

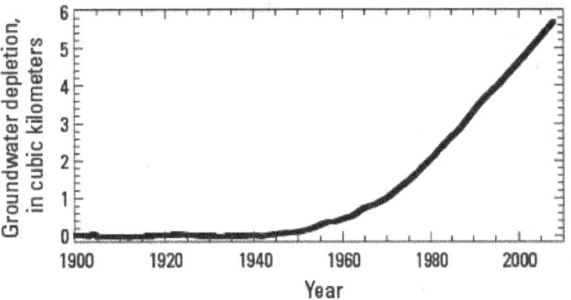

Figure 32.   Cumulative groundwater depletion in the Hueco Bolson, 1900 through 2008.

Las Vegas Valley, Nevada

Las Vegas Valley is located in southern Nevada (figs. 1 and 2). The 4,050 km² area has an arid climate and lies within the Great Basin region of the Basin and Range physiographic province (Wood, 2000). The hydrology and hydrogeologic framework of the area are described in more detail by Plume (1989) and Morgan and Dettinger (1996). The valley-wide average specific yield is about 8 percent (Morgan and Dettinger, 1996).

The first flowing well was drilled in Las Vegas Valley in 1907 (Pavelko and others, 1999). Withdrawal from wells remained fairly constant at a rate of about 0.03 km³/yr from 1912 until 1941, but a significant growth in demand occurred from then through about 1970, when withdrawals peaked at about 0.11 km³/yr (Wood, 2000, fig. 2). Groundwater withdrawals represented 90 percent of water use in 1942, and about 70 percent during 1955-71, but decreased afterwards to about 20 percent of total use during 1989-95 (Wood, 2000). Withdrawals between 1912 and 1981 totaled more than 3.1 km³ (Morgan and Dettinger, 1996). Withdrawals totaled about 4.7 km³ between the years 1935 and 1996. The valley has been in an overdraft condition since soon after groundwater development began, which has led to serious problems of water-level declines, springs drying up, and land subsidence. Withdrawals from the mid-1970s through 1995 were fairly stable at a reduced level averaging about 0.9 km³/yr. Pavelko and others (1999) indicate that about 5 percent of the pumpage between 1907 and 1996 was derived from compaction of the aquifer system—a permanent depletion of about 0.23 km³ of groundwater.

The first phase of the Southern Nevada Water Project (SNWP), established in 1971, permitted large imports of water to the valley from the Colorado River (Morgan and Dettinger, 1996). Imports of water increased from 0.15 km³ in 1980 to

about 0.40 km³ in 1995 (Wood, 2000). Artificial recharge into the principal aquifer began in 1987. As of May 2000, nearly 0.26 km³ had been recharged to the aquifer system in the Las Vegas area, partly ameliorating water-level declines.

Harrill (1976) calculated groundwater depletion on the basis of observed water-level changes and indicates that the storage depletion from predevelopment to 1955 was about 0.83 km³ (Harrill, 1976). From 1955 through 1962, depletion was about 0.32 km³ and during 1963–72 was an additional 0.42 km³. Depletion is about 64 percent of the total pumpage (Harrill, 1976). Assuming that this ratio applied to the 1973–76 period, an additional depletion of 0.23 km³ occurred during that time (Bell, 1981).

Historical rates of water-level declines are reflected in hydrographs available from several sources. Pavelko and others (1999) report that groundwater levels declined at an average rate of about 0.3 m/yr between 1912 and 1944, and that by 1990 some areas had experienced more than 90 m of drawdown. Several well hydrographs show steady continual declines from the 1940s through 1995 (Wood, 2000). However, other well hydrographs show water levels increased substantially from the mid-1970s through 1995 (Wood, 2000). The Southern Nevada Water Authority shows hydrographs for 16 observation wells at 12 sites throughout the valley, generally for the period 2000–2010 (accessed January 5, 2011, from links at *http://www.lasvegasgmp.com/html/telemetry_map.html*). Most of these show water levels rising during this period—at an average rate of about 0.59 m/yr.

A map of water-level declines in the principal aquifer from pre-development conditions to 1990 (Burbey, 1995) and a map of water-level changes in the valley between 1990 and 1995 (Wood, 2000) provide a basis for estimating groundwater depletion. GIS tools were used to estimate depletion volumes as the product of the area-weighted declines and the average specific yield of 0.08. This indicated a total depletion of 2.83 km³ from pre-development to 1990 and a small decrease in depletion volume of about 0.13 km³ between 1990 and 1995, most likely due to decreased withdrawals and new artificial recharge programs. Through 1995, the total depletion volume is therefore 2.7 km³. The available water-level records indicate that the 1990–95 rate of about 0.026 km³/yr would continue through 2008. In estimating the rate of depletion prior to 1955, it is assumed that no depletion occurred before 1912 and that from 1912 through 1955 the rate was proportional to the rate of withdrawal. It is further assumed that a linear trend exists between control points discussed above. This yields an estimated total depletion of 2.3 km³ in 2000 and 2.1 km³ in 2008 (fig. 33; table 1).

Los Angeles Basin, California

The Los Angeles Basin is a heavily populated coastal basin in southern California (figs. 1 and 2) in which four separate groundwater basins have been identified. About one-third of the water consumed by 4 million residents in the Central and West Coast Basins is groundwater (Hillhouse and

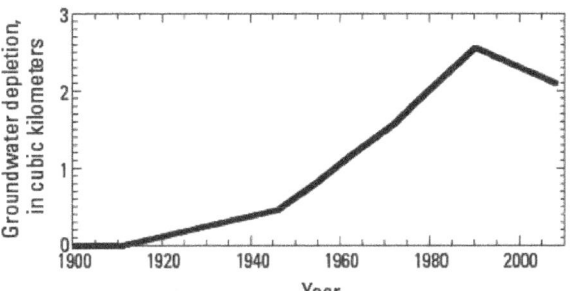

Figure 33. Cumulative groundwater depletion in the Las Vegas Valley, Nevada, 1900 through 2008.

others, 2002). These two basins are the largest and include an area of about 1,200 km². They are underlain by sediments as deep as 450 m below land surface. The hydrogeologic framework is described in detail by Reichard and others (2003). Los Angeles has a Subtropical-Mediterranean climate and an average annual precipitation of about 38.5 cm.

Since the first water wells were drilled in the mid-1800s, groundwater has been a significant component of water supply in the region (Reichard and others, 2003). By the early 1900s more than 4,000 wells were in the study area (Mendenhall, 1905a, 1905b). A flowing well in 1895, located 3.2 km north of Signal Hill, had water levels 24 m above land surface (Poland and others, 1959). Many flowing wells were reported to exist in the area (Mendenhall, 1905a, 1905b). At that time, approximately 30 percent of the area was under flowing artesian conditions (Johnson and Chong, 2005). By 1953, groundwater withdrawals increased to about 0.4 km³/yr (Johnson and Chong, 2005). Historical pumpage is documented for 1935–2000 (Reichard and others, 2003). Groundwater development through the first half of the 20th century resulted in large water-level declines and associated problems such as seawater intrusion and reductions in discharge to wetlands, as well as contributing to land subsidence (Reichard and others, 2003). This led to the adjudication of the basins in the early 1960s and the initiation of groundwater management activities including artificial recharge, pumping restrictions, and importation of surface water. Records of observation wells show that water levels in wells typically declined substantially from the early 1900s through the early 1960s, and then tended to recover to some degree into a new dynamic equilibrium (Reichard and others, 2003; Johnson and Chong, 2005; Water Replenishment District of Southern California, 2010).

The Water Replenishment District of Southern California (WRDSC) calculates and reports the annual and cumulative changes in groundwater storage in the Central and West Coast Basins since 1961. Their analysis (Water Replenishment District of Southern California, 2010) indicates that from 1961 to 2008 the cumulative change in storage was an increase of about 0.20 km³.

The pre-1961 depletion can be estimated two ways. One is based on estimated pumpage. Extrapolation of pumpage curves (Reichard and others, 2003) indicate that the average

annual withdrawal during 1900–61 was about 0.23 km³/yr, for a total cumulative withdrawal of about 13.8 km³. This period is prior to adjudication and implementation of conservation and artificial recharge measures, so it is assumed that the ratio of depletion to withdrawals was approximately the same as in the Central Valley of California. This analogy provides a basis for estimating depletion in the Los Angeles Basin. In the Central Valley, data and analyses indicate that the total cumulative groundwater withdrawals from about 1900 through 1961 was about 128 km³ (Bertoldi and others, 1991) and the total decrease in groundwater storage from predevelopment to 1961 was about 58 km³ (Williamson and others, 1989). Therefore, in the Central Valley, depletion represents about 45 percent of pumpage. Applying this percentage to the Los Angeles Basin study areas indicates that approximately 6.2 km³ of depletion occurred during 1900–61.

A second approach to estimating depletion is based on estimated water-level changes and the storage properties of the aquifer system. A map of water-level declines from 1904 to 2004 (Johnson and Chong, 2005, fig. 4) show that in many areas the decline is greater than 46 m. The average decline over the entire study area is about 25 m. Specific yield in the coastal Los Angeles area ranges from 0.15 to 0.23, and the specific yield of the uppermost model layer ranges from 0.075 to 0.25 (Reichard and others, 2003). For this calculation, it is assumed that the average specific yield is 0.15. Where water-level declines represent primarily a decline in artesian heads, the change in volume of groundwater in storage would be quite small. Thus, as a first approximation it is assumed that all declines in the 30 percent of the study area where flowing wells existed do not contribute materially to the total depletion. Thus, the area over which the average water-level decline would apply is reduced to just 840 km². On this basis, the cumulative depletion through 1961 is estimated to be about 2.52 km³.

There is uncertainty in both of these estimates. For the purposes of this assessment, the average of those two values is used. This results in an estimated depletion during 1900–61 of about 4.4 km³. For the period between 1900 and 1961, it is assumed that the depletion increases from 0.0 to 4.4 km³ at a rate parallel to the fractional water-level declines in observation well 2S/13W–10A1, located in an area of relatively high water-level declines near the north-central edge of the study area (Johnson and Chong, 2005, figs. 3 and 4). For the post-1961 years, it is simply assumed that the estimates of annual storage change computed by WRDSC (2010) can be added to the estimated 1961 value. This results in an estimated cumulative depletion of 4.1 km³ in 2000 and 4.2 km³ in 2008 (fig. 34; table 1).

Mesilla Basin, New Mexico

The Mesilla Basin includes an area of about 2,850 km² and is mostly located in Doña Ana County, south-central New Mexico, but extends into El Paso County, Texas, and Chihuahua, Mexico (figs. 1 and 2). The Mesilla Basin is the

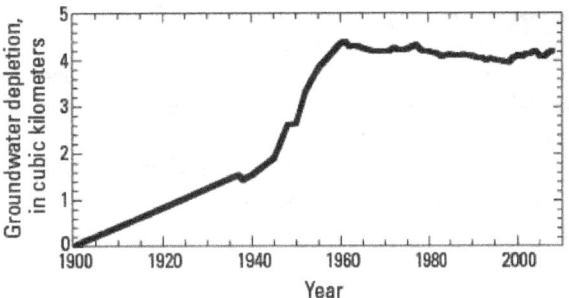

Figure 34. Cumulative groundwater depletion in the Los Angeles Basin, California, 1900 through 2008.

southernmost of the series of basins that run along the Rio Grande in New Mexico, and the basin deposits are in direct hydraulic connection to the river. A number of observation wells in the area show long-term water-level declines of tens of meters (see Frenzel, 1992, fig. 25).

Frenzel and Kaehler (1992) provide a detailed description of the hydrology and groundwater resources in the Mesilla Basin. They note that the climate primarily is arid but becomes semiarid in high, mountainous regions. The average annual precipitation, mostly in the form of rain, in the Las Cruces area for 1851 to 1976 is 21 cm. Pan evaporation averages about 240 cm/yr. The basin is bounded by uplifted blocks of bedrock or by relatively impermeable volcanic rocks and is filled with alluvial sediment from the surrounding mountains and with fluvial sediment deposited by an ancestral Rio Grande. The geology and hydrogeology are described in more detail by Frenzel and Kaehler (1992), Frenzel (1992), and Hawley and others (2001).

The chief use of water in the Mesilla Basin is for agricultural irrigation. As of February 1948, about 70 irrigation wells were in the Rincon and Mesilla Valleys. As of 1975, about 920 usable irrigation wells were in the Mesilla Valley. Groundwater in the basin is generally unconfined (Hawley and others, 2001).

A 3D, transient, groundwater-flow model of the Mesilla Basin was created by Frenzel and Kaehler (1992) and later updated by Frenzel (1992). The updated model used MODFLOW (McDonald and Harbaugh, 1988) to simulate steady-state predevelopment conditions (pre-1915) and transient conditions from 1915 through 1985. The model included 4 layers, 36 rows, and 64 columns of cells, and each cell ranged in size from 0.8 to 3.2 km on a side. Twenty-two irregularly spaced stress periods were used in the 70-year simulation period. The specific storage for the model was estimated to be 3.3×10^{-6} m^{-1}, and the specific yield was estimated to be 0.20 (dimensionless). Other assumptions, hydraulic properties, boundary conditions, and calibration methods are described in more detail by Frenzel (1992).

Model calibration was based on comparisons of calculated heads with observed data. Over the total simulation time (1915–85), the model indicated a total groundwater depletion of about 0.30 km^3. Long-term water-level records from several

key monitoring wells in the valley (downloaded from the U.S. Geological Survey National Water Information System at *http://waterdata.usgs.gov/nm/nwis/current/?type=gw*) show no substantial water-level changes from 1985 to 1997, but during 1998–2008 steady declines were on the order of several meters. On this basis, it is assumed that there was no additional depletion from 1986 through 1997, but that from 1998 through 2008 the depletion continued at the same rate as calculated for the final 7-year stress period of the model study—a rate of about 0.01 km^3/yr. The estimated total groundwater depletion from 1900 through 2000 is about 0.3 km^3 and from 1900 through 2008 is about 0.4 km^3 (fig. 35, table 1).

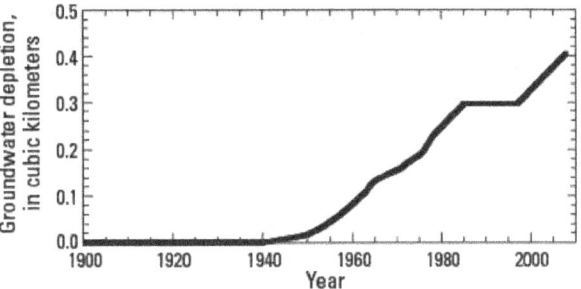

Figure 35. Cumulative groundwater depletion in the Mesilla Basin, New Mexico, 1900 through 2008.

Middle Rio Grande Basin, New Mexico

The Middle Rio Grande Basin encompasses about 7,900 km^2 in central New Mexico (Bartolino and Cole, 2002) (figs. 1 and 2). The groundwater resources of the Middle Rio Grande Basin are described in detail by Bartolino and Cole (2002); most of the following description of the basin is taken directly from that report.

Much of the Middle Rio Grande Basin is classified as desert, with mean annual precipitation ranging from 19 cm at Belen to 32 cm at Cochiti Dam. In the Middle Rio Grande Basin, the surface water and groundwater systems are closely linked. The most prominent hydrologic feature in the basin is the Rio Grande, which flows through the entire length of the basin, generally from north to south.

The Middle Rio Grande Basin lies in the Rio Grande rift valley. Basin-fill deposits range in thickness from about 430 m at the basin margins to approximately 4,270 m in the deepest parts of the Middle Rio Grande Basin. The hydrogeologic framework is discussed in more detail by Bartolino and Cole (2002).

A groundwater-level map showing conditions in the winter of 1994–95 shows well-defined cones of depression in the Albuquerque and Rio Rancho areas and marked distortion of water-level contours across the Albuquerque area (Tiedeman and others, 1998). A groundwater-level map of predevelopment conditions in the Middle Rio Grande Basin was constructed using a number of sources (Bexfield and

Anderholm, 2000). Long-term hydrographs from a number of observation wells in the study area reflect the range of water-level changes in the basin (Bartolino and Cole, 2002).

The difference between the predevelopment water levels and the 1995 water levels reflect the long-term groundwater depletion in the aquifer system. A map of water-level declines for the Albuquerque area from predevelopment to 2002 (Bexfield and Anderholm, 2000) shows that water levels declined by more than 30 m in an area of more than 65 km². During 1995, about 0.4 km³ of groundwater was withdrawn for various uses in the basin (Wilson and Lucero, 1997). About 55 percent of the groundwater withdrawals were for public water supply.

Several groundwater-flow models of the Middle Rio Grande Basin have been developed. A recent 3D model (McAda and Barroll, 2002) uses MODFLOW-2000 (Harbaugh and others, 2000) to simulate the system for predevelopment steady-state conditions and transient conditions from 1900 through 2000. The model uses a total of 52 stress periods for the entire 100-year simulation period. The model consists of nine layers that get increasingly thicker with depth (McAda and Barroll, 2002). Each layer is divided into a grid of cells containing 156 rows and 80 columns, and each cell is 1 km on a side. Specific storage was estimated to be 6.6×10^{-6} m^{-1} in the model. Specific yield was estimated to be 0.2 (dimensionless). The other conceptualizations, hydraulic properties, boundary conditions, and the calibration process for the model are discussed in detail by McAda and Barroll (2002).

The calibrated model computes a water budget for the aquifer system, which shows that changes in aquifer storage were small until about 1950 and then increased noticeably. In 1999, the rate of depletion of aquifer storage was about 0.074 km³/yr. In 2000 the cumulative net depletion since predevelopment times was about 2.4 km³. The withdrawal rates have decreased since 2000, so the depletion rates should also be reduced accordingly (D.P. McAda, written commun., 2010). Assuming that the 5-year average rate of depletion during 1995 through 2000 (0.0837 km³/yr) was reduced to half that rate during 2001 through 2008, then the cumulative groundwater depletion from 1900 through 2008 is about 2.7 km³ (fig. 36; table 1).

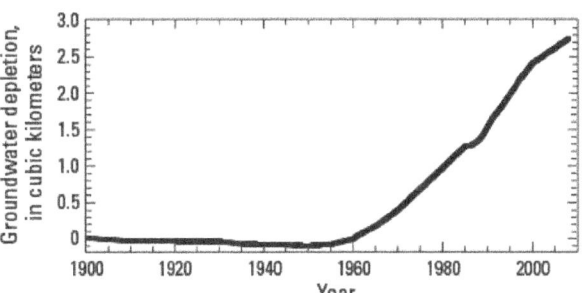

Figure 36.   Cumulative groundwater depletion in the Middle Rio Grande Basin, New Mexico, 1900 through 2008.

Milford Area, Utah

The Milford area in southwestern Utah includes about 3,000 km² in the northern part of the Escalante Valley (figs. 1 and 2). Groundwater occurs in unconsolidated valley fill deposits, mostly under water-table conditions. Water levels have declined steadily since the 1950s, largely in response to increasing pumpage during that period (Sandberg, 1964). These declines continued through 2002, resulting from continued large groundwater withdrawals for irrigation (Slaugh, 2002).

The Milford area of the Escalante Desert lies in the Basin and Range physiographic province. Climate of the Milford area varies from semiarid on the basin floor to subhumid at higher altitudes in the surrounding mountains. The average annual precipitation (1952–2001) near Milford is about 23 cm (Slaugh, 2002). Average pan evaporation in the Milford area for April–October during 1953–71 was 198 cm (Mower and Cordova, 1974). The hydrology and related aspects of the Milford area are described in detail by Mower and Cordova (1974) and Mason (1998).

The Milford area is underlain by consolidated rocks ranging from Precambrian to Quaternary age and by unconsolidated basin fill deposits. The latter are about 1.5 to 1.8 km thick and constitute the primary groundwater system. The groundwater is unconfined along the margins of the basin but becomes confined in the center of the southern half of the basin (Mason, 1998). Mower and Cordova (1974) reported specific yield values ranging from 0.04 for clayey silt to 0.2 for sandy gravel.

Recharge occurs from adjacent mountain fronts, from seepage losses along irrigation canals, and from infiltration of excess applied irrigation water. A major source of groundwater discharge is by evapotranspiration. Well withdrawals are mostly for irrigation and increased steadily from the early 1930s through the late 1970s (fig. 37), with the biggest increases starting after 1949 (Slaugh, 2002, fig. 29). The long-term average withdrawal during 1931–2001 is about 0.05 km³/yr. Associated with the groundwater withdrawals and reduction in storage are water-level declines. The water levels continued to decline after the early 1980s through 2002 (Slaugh, 2002).

A 3D groundwater-flow model for the Milford area was developed by Mason (1998) using MODFLOW (McDonald and Harbaugh, 1988). The model included two layers for a steady-state flow model used to simulate predevelopment conditions. The model was calibrated to approximate steady-state conditions for 1927, before groundwater development began.

A third layer was added to the model when developing a transient flow model to represent conditions during 1950–82 (Mason, 1998). For this model, it was assumed that steady-state conditions prevailed in the Milford area until 1950, when groundwater withdrawals began to increase rapidly (Mason, 1998, p. 20). The transient simulation period is divided into seven stress periods of irregular duration that represent years of similar groundwater withdrawal rates. For the period from

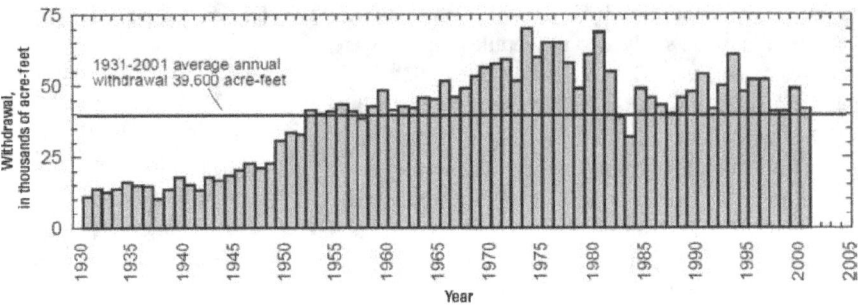

Figure 37. Annual withdrawal from wells in the Milford area (from Slaugh, 2002, fig. 29). Long-term average withdrawal rate is about 0.05 km³/yr.

1950 through 1982, the total net depletion of groundwater storage calculated by the calibrated transient model was 0.67 km³.

Records of wells in the area show that groundwater levels generally declined during 1982–2000. The long-term hydrographs for 10 wells (Slaugh, 2002, fig. 28) were used as a basis for extrapolating model results through the year 2000 and beyond. The average water-level decline from March 1983 through March 2001 was about 58 percent of that from the earliest record for each of the 10 wells through March 1983. This same percentage is applied to the cumulative groundwater depletion computed by the model through 1982 (0.66 km³). On this basis, there would be an additional 0.38 km³ of depletion during 1983–2000. Therefore, the total groundwater depletion in the Milford area during the 20th century was approximately 1.0 km³. Extrapolating this same rate through 2008 indicates a total net depletion for 1900–2008 of about 1.2 km³ (fig. 38; table 1)

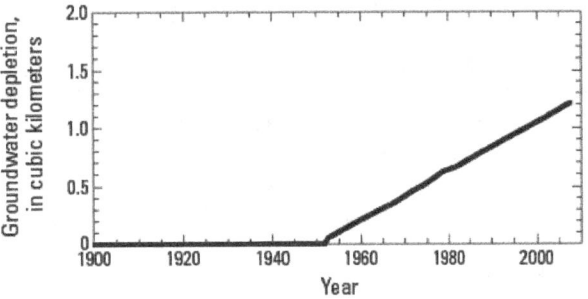

Figure 38. Cumulative groundwater depletion in the Milford area, Utah, 1900 through 2008.

Mimbres Basin, New Mexico

The Mimbres Basin is a closed basin in southwestern New Mexico that has an area of about 13,300 km² (figs. 1 and 2). Climate in the basin is arid to semiarid, with a mean annual precipitation ranging from less than 23 cm in the southern part to more than 61 cm in the mountains (Hanson and others, 1994). Groundwater levels in the Mimbres Basin have declined since the pumping of groundwater for irrigation of crops began in the early 1900s (Hanson and others, 1994). By 1975, 0.14 km³/yr of groundwater was being withdrawn in the

basin. A hydrograph for a well near Deming shows a steady decline of about 12 m from 1930 through 1980 (Hanson and others, 1994). Water levels east of Columbus declined more than 40 m from 1910 to 1970. The average specific yield of the sediments is 0.14 (Hanson and others, 1994).

A two-dimensional transient model of the valley-fill aquifer in the basin was developed and calibrated for the period 1930–85 by Hanson and others (1994) using the code of Trescott and others (1976) and MODFLOW (McDonald and Harbaugh, 1988). The grid included 56 rows and 46 columns with a variable spacing that ranged from 1,860 m to 6,276 m on a side (Hanson and others, 1994). Additional details about the model characteristics and the calibration process are presented by Hanson and others (1994). The results indicated that most (77 percent) of the water pumped by 1985 was derived from storage. The total net depletion of storage during 1931–85 was 3.28 km³. The depletion was greatest during 1971–75 and decreased by almost a factor of two during 1981–85. The historical rate of depletion during this time period was estimated by assuming that transient changes in depletion were proportional to the net groundwater withdrawals during 1931–85, for which data are available in 5-year increments (Hanson and others, 1994).

Recent analysis and model results show observed and simulated water-level declines in a number of observation wells (Balleau Groundwater, Inc., 2009). In general, these show water levels continuing to decline from 1986 through 1999 at about the same rate as was observed during the previous several years. However, water levels were generally stable from 2000 through 2008. On this basis, the depletion volumes through 2008 are extrapolated by applying the 1980–85 rate of depletion of 0.067 km³/yr to 1986–99. This results (fig. 39; table 1) in an estimated cumulative groundwater depletion since 1900 of 4.2 km³ in both 2000 and 2008.

Mojave River Basin, California

The Mojave River groundwater basin is located in the western part of the Mojave Desert, about 130 km northeast of Los Angeles, California (Stamos and others, 2001b) (figs. 1 and 2). The groundwater basin has an area of about 3,600 km² and has an arid climate (mean annual precipitation is less than 15 cm) (Stamos and others, 2001a). Groundwater is the primary source of water supply, which has resulted in an overdraft condition (Stamos and others, 2001b). To help mitigate

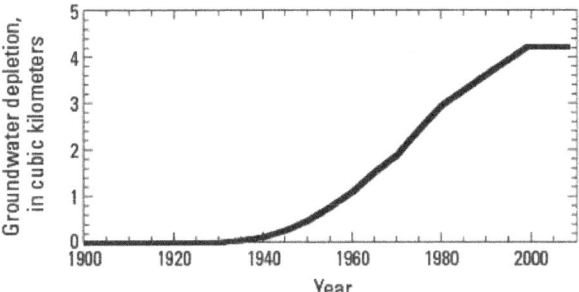

Figure 39. Cumulative groundwater depletion in the Mimbres Basin, New Mexico, 1900 through 2008.

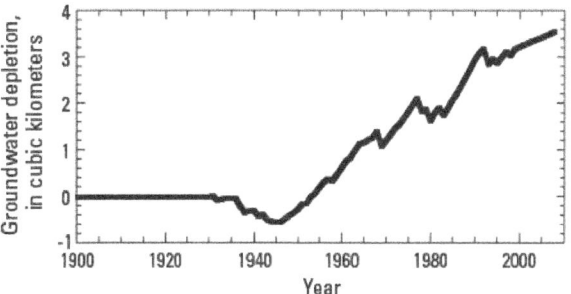

Figure 40. Cumulative groundwater depletion in the Mojave River Basin, California, 1900 through 2008.

the problem, at least partly, the Mojave Water Agency began a practice of artificial recharge using imported water.

The aquifer system consists of unconsolidated alluvium. The hydrogeologic framework is described in detail by Stamos and others (2003). Groundwater development started before the late 1880s (Stamos and others, 2001a). Annual pumpage data for 1931–99 show that withdrawals increased steeply from the mid-1940s through the late 1950s, and then gradually increased more until about 1990, after which it gradually diminished by 1999 to about 70 percent of its peak value of about 0.3 km³/yr in 1989 (Stamos and others, 2001a).

A 3D, transient groundwater-flow model of the area was developed and documented by Stamos and others (2001a) using MODFLOW (McDonald and Harbaugh, 1988). The model included 2 layers, 161 rows, and 200 columns of cells with a horizontal grid spacing of 610 m on a side. An initial steady-state simulation was calibrated to represent predevelopment conditions prior to 1931, and then a transient simulation was applied to 1931–99. Additional details about the model and its calibration are presented by Stamos and others (2001a).

The model results indicate that the amount of groundwater in storage generally increased slightly through the mid-1940s, but then decreased substantially after that until about 1990, when the rate of depletion slowed. By 1999, the cumulative depletion from storage was about 3.2 km³. During the last 5 years of the simulation, the average rate of depletion was 0.041 km³/yr. Assuming that this rate, which is much lower than the long-term average rate, applies through 2008, it is calculated that the total depletion in 2000 was 3.2 km³ and in 2008 was 3.6 km³ (fig. 40; table 1).

Pahvant Valley, Utah

The Pahvant Valley includes about 780 km² southeast of the Sevier Desert in central Utah (Mower, 1964) (figs. 1 and 2). Groundwater withdrawals in the valley are used primarily for irrigation and have led to long-term water-level declines. The climate is characterized as semiarid on the basin floor to subhumid at the higher altitudes in the mountains. Average annual precipitation in the valley was 38.4 cm between 1931 and 2001 (Swenson, 2002). Pan evaporation in the lower

altitudes of the Pahvant Valley and adjacent areas is estimated to be 178 cm (Holmes and Thiros, 1990).

The area lies in the Great Basin section of the Basin and Range province in the western United States. The primary aquifer in Pahvant Valley consists of lacustrine and alluvial deposits of gravel, sand, and silt. The water-bearing units are interbedded with clays and basalts in the central part of the study area. A more detailed description of the hydrology and hydrogeology of the region is presented by Holmes and Thiros (1990).

Natural recharge to the aquifer system in the Pahvant Valley occurs principally along the east side of the valley from direct precipitation on the Pahvant Range and Canyon Mountains, seepage from streams, and minor subsurface inflow from the nearby Milford area. Recharge also comes from infiltration of irrigation water and seepage from irrigation canals. Surface water from the Sevier River has been imported to the study area by the Central Utah Canal since 1934 (Mower, 1965).

The first irrigation wells in the area were drilled in 1915. Significant quantities of water are now withdrawn from the aquifer system in the Pahvant Valley from pumped and flowing wells (fig. 41). Swenson (2002) shows annual withdrawals from 1946 through 2001 averaged about 0.1 km³/yr during 1990–2000. From the early 1950s to 1982, groundwater levels generally declined as a result of below average annual precipitation and increased withdrawal. Precipitation from 1982 to 1985 was significantly above average and groundwater withdrawals were subsequently lower. Water levels generally rose to above the levels in the early 1950s. Since 1985, water levels have again declined with continued large withdrawals for irrigation (Swenson, 2002).

A 3D groundwater-flow model for the Pahvant Valley was developed by Holmes and Thiros (1990) using MODFLOW (McDonald and Harbaugh, 1988). Steady-state conditions were assumed for the period prior to 1947 when discharge and water levels were fairly stable. A transient simulation of subsequent conditions used 39 yearly stress periods to represent the time period from 1947 to 1985 (inclusive). The model consisted of 4 layers, 58 rows, and 35 columns with cell areas ranging from 0.65 km² to 11.1 km².

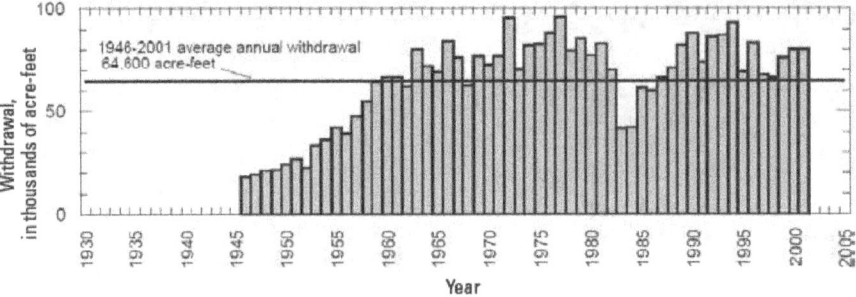

Figure 41. Annual withdrawals from wells in the Pahvant Valley (modified from Swenson, 2002, fig. 23). Long-term average withdrawal rate is about 0.08 km³/yr.

A cumulative groundwater budget was computed for every time step during the transient run of the groundwater model. The total loss of groundwater from storage was calculated from the cumulative volumetric groundwater budget as the difference between groundwater added into storage and groundwater removed from storage in the aquifer. For the entire simulation period, the model calculated a net depletion of 0.48 km³.

Water levels in the Pahvant Valley generally declined in two separate time periods during the developmental history of the aquifer system—one period began in the early 1950s and lasted until the early to mid-1980s, and a second period of decline was from the mid- to late 1980s through 2002. Depletion after 1985 was estimated by extrapolation—assuming a correlation of depletion to average water-level changes in wells. Therefore, it was assumed that (1) the volume of groundwater in storage increased during 1986–87 at the same rate as calculated for 1984–85 (0.063 km³/yr), (2) no change occurred during 1988, and (3) from 1999 through 2008, depletion increased at the same rate as the average rate computed by the model during 1960–80 (0.037 km³/yr). On this basis, it is estimated that the cumulative net groundwater depletion from 1900 through 2000 is about 0.8 km³ and about 1.1 km³ from 1900 through 2008 (fig. 42; table 1).

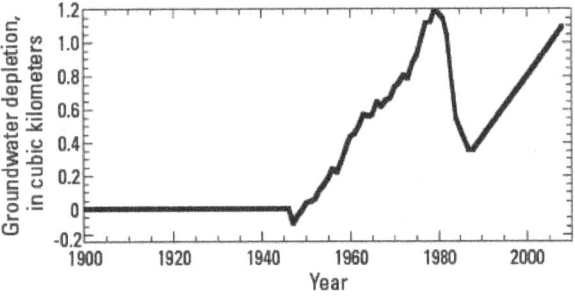

Figure 42. Cumulative groundwater depletion in the Pahvant Valley, Utah, 1900 through 2008.

Paradise Valley, Nevada

Paradise Valley is a basin tributary to the Humboldt River in north-central Nevada (figs. 1 and 2). Paradise Valley extends about 64 km northward from the Humboldt River

near Winnemucca and includes an area of about 850 km². The climate is arid to semiarid and has large diurnal fluctuations in temperature (Prudic and Herman, 1996). Annual average precipitation at the town of Paradise Valley in the northern end of the valley is 24 cm for 1955–82 and at Winnemucca was 20 cm during the same period. The groundwater flow system in the valley was analyzed by Prudic and Herman (1996), who note that increased groundwater pumping in the valley in the 1970s caused water-table declines of as much as 25 m.

As described by Prudic and Herman (1996), the major aquifer consists of basin fill deposits—mostly unconsolidated alluvium. The maximum thickness of the basin fill exceeds 2,400 m in the center of the valley. The specific yield of the basin fill deposits varies with lithology and location. Clay deposits have an estimated specific yield of 6 percent, whereas sands have a reported value of 30 percent (Prudic and Herman, 1996).

Most of the readily available groundwater in the valley occurs in unconsolidated deposits under both unconfined and confined conditions. Groundwater pumpage in the valley was small prior to 1948, and then gradually increased. Use of irrigation wells, however, increased substantially during the 1970s. Total pumpage during 1981 in Paradise Valley was about 0.06 km³/yr.

The groundwater flow system in Paradise Valley was simulated by Prudic and Herman (1996) with a 3D, three-layer, transient, MODFLOW model (McDonald and Harbaugh, 1988). The grid consisted of 33 columns and 89 rows of cells that were about 762 m on a side. Three layers were used to represent the basin-fill aquifer vertically. Predevelopment conditions were simulated first as steady-state conditions. This provided the basis for a transient model to simulate the effects of development during 1948 through 1982. A more detailed description of the model and its calibration is presented by Prudic and Herman (1996).

The groundwater model calculates a cumulative groundwater budget for the entire simulation period. For the period from 1968 through 1982, the calculated total net depletion of groundwater storage was 0.136 km³ (Prudic and Herman, 1996).

Recent water-level monitoring in one key observation well in Humboldt County (data downloaded July 19, 2010, from *http://nwis.waterdata.usgs.gov/nv/nwis/gwlevels*) indicates that water-level declines, and hence depletion, during 1982–2008 was approximately equal to that during 1962–82.

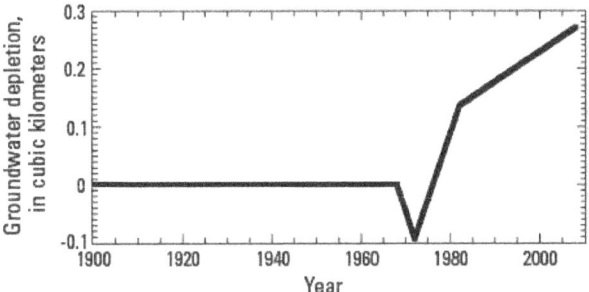

Figure 43. Cumulative groundwater depletion in Paradise Valley, Nevada, 1900 through 2008.

On the basis of this extrapolation, the total depletion in 2000 is about 0.23 km³ and by 2008 is about 0.27 km³ (fig. 43; table 1).

Pecos River Basin, Texas

The Cenozoic Pecos River Basin alluvial aquifer covers roughly 13,000 km² in western Texas (Ryder, 1996) (figs. 1 and 2). Groundwater is primarily used for irrigation, and groundwater was the source of 94 percent of the water used in the region by 1995 (Boghici, 1999). Water-level declines of more than 60 m were observed in the aquifer in parts of Reeves County and Pecos County (Jones, 2001). Legislation was passed in 1985 in Texas to examine aquifers in the State with critical groundwater problems—one such aquifer being the Cenozoic Pecos River Basin alluvial aquifer.

The aquifer occurs in a region with an arid climate. Precipitation ranges from 23 to 33 cm per year, falls mostly from late spring to early fall, and is greater in the eastern part of the study area (Ashworth, 1990; Boghici, 1999). Pan evaporation rates average around 200 cm per year (Ashworth, 1990). The Pecos River runs from northwest to the southeast across the study area (Ryder, 1996).

The aquifer consists of thick and extensive alluvium, with the thickest deposits occurring in two separate troughs. The overlying terrain is characterized by flat to rolling plains that slope gently towards the Pecos River. Extensive sand dunes, originating from Pleistocene aeolian deposits, overlie the alluvium in the eastern part of the study area (Jones, 2001). The alluvium is mostly composed of unconsolidated or poorly cemented clay, sand, gravel, and caliche of Tertiary and Quaternary age. The thickness of the alluvial deposits typically ranges from 30 to 90 m, but is as much as 460 m in places (Ryder, 1996). Ashworth (1990) provides a more detailed description of the hydrogeology of the Cenozoic Pecos alluvial aquifer.

Water-level fluctuations in the aquifer have been associated with the varying intensity of irrigation pumpage throughout the development of the Cenozoic Pecos alluvial aquifer. Significant development began in the 1940s and peaked in the 1950s as the number of irrigation wells in Reeves County alone increased from 35 to 355 between 1940

and 1950 (Jones, 2001). The first irrigation well was drilled in Pecos County in 1948, and approximately 250 wells were in use in the county by 1958. The aquifer had experienced water-level declines of more than 60 m in south-central Reeves and northwest Pecos Counties by the end of this time period (Jones, 2001).

Groundwater development and water-table levels stabilized in the 1960s, and water levels began to recover in the mid-1970s as irrigation pumping decreased. By the 1990s, the parts of Reeves County that were heavily impacted by irrigation pumpage showed a significant rise in groundwater levels. Declines, however, were still observed in the Coyanosa area of Reeves and Pecos Counties and were attributed to continued irrigation, public supply, and industrial use (Jones, 2001). Total withdrawals from the alluvium increased from 0.18 km³ in 1985 to 0.22 km³ in 1995—mostly used for irrigation (Boghici, 1999). The cumulative volume of groundwater pumpage in both Reeves and Pecos Counties during 1940–2000 is about 24.9 km³.

Groundwater depletion was estimated using a water-budget approach. The available aquifer storage volume of 11.7 km³ in 1976–80 (Muller and Price, 1979) was used as the basis and starting point for estimating total storage depletion throughout the development history of the aquifer. Depletion was estimated for selected years by subtracting annual groundwater pumpage (Hood and Knowles, 1952, table 1; Ogilbee and others, 1962, table 3; Texas Water Development Board, 2001, table 1) from the average annual effective recharge (Boghici, 1999). The total cumulative groundwater depletion from 1940 (representing predevelopment conditions) to 2000 was thus estimated to be approximately 20.2 km³, noting that most of the depletion in aquifer storage occurred between 1950 and 1980.

A cross-check was done by also estimating groundwater depletion on the basis of water-level data, changes in saturated thickness, and estimates of specific yield. The areas in south-central Reeves County and northern Pecos County, where the two cones of depression were observed, were examined. GIS tools were used to construct maps of water-table changes between 1947 and 1998 for Reeves County and from predevelopment conditions to 1998 for Pecos County from existing maps (Armstrong and McMillion, 1961; Ogilbee and others, 1962; Jones, 2001). A specific yield of 0.10 is reported for the alluvium in Reeves and Pecos Counties (Muller and Price, 1979). Total depletion volumes of 5.3 km³ and 19.2 km³ were computed in Pecos and Reeves Counties, respectively. Thus, the total groundwater depletion in the Cenozoic Pecos alluvial aquifer from 1947 to 1998 is estimated to equal 24.5 km³, which is about 20 percent greater than the amount estimated using the water-budget approach and exceeds the estimated pumpage. Therefore, the former estimate is taken to be more reliable. Considering the uncertainties and simplifying assumptions that underlie both calculations, this discrepancy is relatively small and not surprising.

During the 16-year period (1984–2000) that includes the last three calculated values of depletion, depletion showed a nearly steady, gradual, linear rate of increased depletion of about 0.093 km³/yr. Assuming this rate continues through 2008, the rate yields an estimated total groundwater depletion in 2008 of 21.0 km³ (fig. 44; table 1).

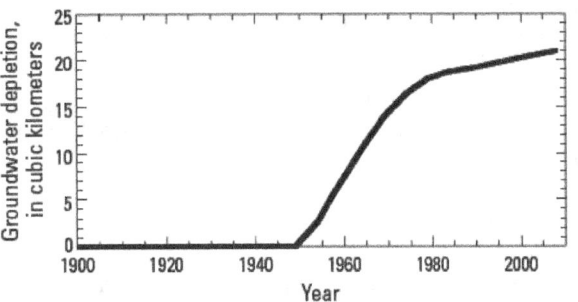

Figure 44.   Cumulative groundwater depletion in the Pecos River alluvial aquifer, Texas, 1900 through 2008.

San Luis Valley, Colorado

The San Luis Valley of south-central Colorado is a large intermontane structural basin filled with as much as 9 km of alluvial and lacustrine sediments, interbedded with volcanic flows and tuffs (Emery, 1979) (figs. 1 and 2). The valley includes an area of about 8,300 km² and has an arid climate, with an average annual precipitation of about 19 cm (Emery, 1979). Nearly 2,800 km² of the valley are irrigated by surface water from the Rio Grande and its tributaries, and by groundwater from the valley's extensive unconfined and confined aquifers.

Cultivation of crops became extensive in the 1890s, after the discovery of artesian water (Emery, 1979). By 1904 there were more than 3,200 flowing wells, by 1916 there were 5,000, and in the late 1970s there were nearly 7,700 wells withdrawing water from the confined (artesian) aquifer (Emery, 1979). In addition to wells completed in the confined aquifer, by the late 1970s there were also about 2,300 pumped wells in the unconfined aquifer. This extensive development using both surface water and groundwater sources for irrigation led to a number of problems, including rising water tables and waterlogging in some areas, and declining groundwater levels and depletion in other areas.

To help analyze the groundwater flow system in the San Luis Valley, a 3D electric analog model was developed and calibrated by Emery and others (1975). A 3D digital model of the same area was subsequently developed by Hearne and Dewey (1988). The water budgets computed by both models indicated that from 1950 through 1969, 0.90 km³ of groundwater had been depleted from storage, and during 1970–80 an additional 1.48 km³ had been removed from storage. In total, during 1950–80 a total of 2.38 km³ had been removed from storage in both the confined and unconfined aquifers of the San Luis Valley, Colorado.

Because of a paucity of data, and because recharge and water-table rises from surface-water irrigation offset drawdown due to pumpage, it is assumed that there was no substantial net groundwater depletion prior to 1950. After 1980, records of water-level changes in a number of wells are available from links on the Web site of the U.S. Geological Survey (accessed February 17, 2011, from *http://groundwaterwatch.usgs.gov/StateMaps/CO.html*). A subset of records from wells with long-term data (from before 1980 through 2010) in the four counties in the study area were examined. Of the 18 well records examined in detail, 10 had records starting prior to 1970. Five wells showed no long-term change in water level, but 13 showed substantial declines from the 1970s to 2008. In most cases, the declines were fairly steady, but in a few cases, the rate of decline was noticeably steepest during 2001–05. Overall, it is reasonable to assume that depletion continued after 1980. Assuming that depletion continued at the lower rate of 0.045 km³/yr computed for the period 1950–69, the total cumulative depletion of groundwater from storage from 1900 through 2000 is about 3.3 km³ and from 1900 through 2008 is about 3.6 km³ (fig. 45; table 1).

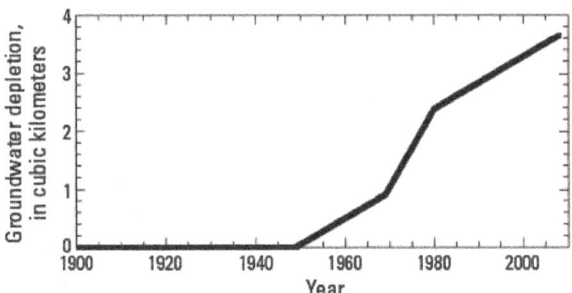

Figure 45.   Cumulative groundwater depletion in the San Luis Valley, Colorado, 1900 through 2008.

Tularosa Basin, New Mexico

The Tularosa Basin includes approximately 17,000 km² in south-central New Mexico (figs. 1 and 2). The aquifer system consists of unconsolidated basin-fill deposits and has been the main source of water in this closed basin. The Tularosa Basin has an arid to semiarid continental climate, with a median annual precipitation in Alamogordo of 28.3 cm (Huff, 2005). Lake evaporation near Alamogordo is approximately 190 cm/yr. Precipitation in the surrounding mountains is approximately twice that of precipitation on the basin floor (Huff, 2005).

The basin is a downfaulted intermountain closed basin formed by faulting along the southern Rio Grande Rift. The basin fill consists of eroded material from the surrounding uplifted terrain and fluvial deposits of the ancestral Rio Grande (Huff, 2005). Unconsolidated coarse- to fine-grained coalescing alluvial-fan deposits rim the basin and grade into finer grained alluvial, fluvial, and lacustrine deposits towards the basin center (Orr and Myers, 1986). McLean (1970) and Orr and Myers (1986) describe the hydrogeology of the Tularosa Basin in more detail.

During development of the region, the greatest consumers of groundwater were agricultural irrigation and the city of Alamogordo, White Sands Missile Range, and Holloman Air Force Base (McLean, 1970). In 1948, an average of about 2,000 m³/d of groundwater were withdrawn for public supply and about 26,000 m³/d for irrigation. By 1995, this increased to 19,000 and 64,000 m³/d, respectively (Huff, 2005). As of 1995, agricultural irrigation accounted for about 58 percent of total groundwater withdrawals in the Tularosa Basin (Huff, 2005).

A 3D steady-state and transient groundwater-flow model for the basin-fill aquifer in the Tularosa Basin was developed by Huff (2005) using MODFLOW-96 (Harbaugh and McDonald, 1996). The model grid includes 81 rows, 50 columns, and 6 layers. A steady-state simulation was calibrated using predevelopment data from Meinzer and Hare (1915). The transient model was calibrated for the period from 1948 to 1995 and the simulation was extended through 2040 based on forecasts of future withdrawal rates. Assumptions, hydraulic properties, boundary conditions, and calibration methods are discussed in more detail by Huff (2005).

To account for uncertainties in the volume of groundwater depleted by agricultural and municipal withdrawals, the model was used to simulate both maximum and zero return-flow scenarios. Under the maximum return-flow scenario, agricultural withdrawals were reduced to represent a net withdrawal in the presence of increased recharge. For the zero return-flow scenario, it was assumed that all water pumped from the aquifer system would be consumed and all water not withdrawn from the aquifer system would leave the basin by evapotranspiration or leakage to the Hueco Bolson aquifer to the south.

Simulated water-level changes between 1948 and 1995 were as large as 30 m for the zero return-flow scenario and 15 m under the maximum return-flow scenario. According to output from the calibrated model, total groundwater depletion for the Tularosa basin-fill aquifer ranges from 1.0 km³ under the zero return-flow scenario to 0.43 km³ under the maximum return-flow scenario. Based on these results, the total groundwater depletion is estimated at 0.72 km³ over the period 1900–95, which represents the average of the depletions calculated for the two end-member return-flow scenarios. During the model's predictive phase, the average rate of depletion for the two return-flow scenarios is 0.0574 km³/yr. Assuming this rate applies after 1995 indicates an estimated cumulative groundwater depletion from 1900 through 2000 of 1.1 km³ and from 1900 through 2008 of 1.5 km³ (fig. 46; table 1).

Western Alluvial Basins: Total

The western United States includes multiple alluvial basins, which often provide substantial quantities of groundwater for local and regional supplies. Data availability

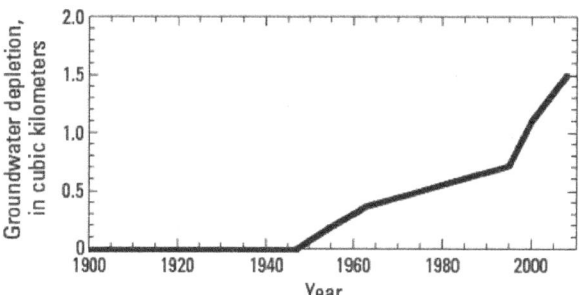

Figure 46. Cumulative groundwater depletion in the Tularosa Basin, New Mexico, 1900 through 2008.

facilitated the estimation of long-term groundwater depletion in 19 of these basins or areas (some, such as Arizona, include several separate basins that are combined in this analysis). In total, these basins account for about 178 km³ of depletion from 1900 through 2008 (table 1), which represents about 22 percent of the total depletion in the United States. The Arizona alluvial basins are the single largest contributor to total depletion in the Western States alluvial basins—comprising about 57 percent of the total alluvial basin depletion.

Western Volcanic Aquifer Systems

Columbia Plateau Aquifer System

The Columbia Plateau aquifer system in the northwestern United States underlies 131,000 km² of southeastern Washington, northeastern Oregon, and northwestern Idaho (Cline and Collins, 1992) (figs. 1 and 2). It is a productive agricultural area, and a large quantity of water used in the region is derived from local and imported surface-water sources. Groundwater usage is substantial, however, and the Columbia Plateau aquifer system is the primary source of groundwater in the region (Hansen and others, 1994). The aquifer system mostly includes the Columbia River Basalt Group and relatively minor amounts of Miocene and Holocene-age interbedded and overlying sediments. Conceptually, the system is a series of productive basalt aquifers consisting of permeable interflow zones separated by less permeable flow interiors; in places, a sedimentary (overburden) aquifer overlies the basalts (Kahle and others, 2011). The volume of the aquifer system is approximately 143,000 km³, 99.3 percent of which is composed of basalt aquifers and 0.7 percent overburden aquifer (Burns and others, 2011).

Water levels in localized areas within the Columbia Plateau aquifer system have risen as much as 90 m due to recharge from surface-water imports in areas of heavy irrigation. Groundwater pumping in areas where surface-water imports are not widely used has led to water-level declines of up to about 90 m (U.S. Geological Survey, 2008). Approximately 80 percent of groundwater withdrawals are used for irrigation purposes, and the remainder is primarily used for municipal and industrial supply.

The major use of water withdrawn in the Columbia Plateau region is for irrigation purposes, and most of the irrigation in the region is supplied by local and imported surface waters. Between 1945 and 1984, about 70 percent of the total water withdrawals were from surface-water sources (Cline and Collins, 1992), and that proportion increased to about 74 percent between 1985 and 2007 (Kahle and others, 2011). The water added to the aquifer from percolation of excess irrigation water has significantly expanded the saturated zones in the overburden aquifer and the uppermost permeable basalt unit, which has raised groundwater levels in these areas close to the land surface (Hansen and others, 1994).

Changes in pump technology and the switch from flood irrigation to sprinkler irrigation greatly increased groundwater use. Nearly 0.22 km^3/yr of groundwater was pumped during 1960; nearly 1.2 km^3/yr was pumped during 1979 (Cline and Collins, 1992). About 1.4 km^3/yr was pumped on average between 1984 and 2007 (Kahle and others, 2011).

Water levels rose an average of 12 m in the overburden aquifer, and water-level rises were as great as 60 m in areas of heavy irrigation by 1985, though water-rises had stabilized in many areas between the mid-1960s and 1970s. Declines in water levels, however, occurred in much of the deeper basalt units. Water-level records for selected wells showing more recent trends indicate that the rates of change of water levels (and therefore of storage volume) were often relatively linear from the 1970s through 2000 (for example, see Snyder and Haynes, 2010, fig. 1).

A groundwater-flow model of the Columbia Plateau aquifer system was developed and documented (Hansen and others, 1994; Vaccaro, 1999). The regional-scale model used MODFLOW (McDonald and Harbaugh, 1988) and included 76 rows, 130 columns, and 5 layers in the grid. The grid spacing was spatially variable. An average specific yield of 0.04 was assumed. A steady-state simulation was created to represent predevelopment conditions for the year 1850, which is assumed to be the most recent year without any water-development activities (although development was negligible to small prior to 1950). A second simulation was based on the average hydrologic conditions during the 2-year period beginning in the spring of 1983 and ending in the spring of 1985.

Based on the differences in the computed water levels for the two models, it was estimated that 12.3 km^3 of water was added to storage in the overburden aquifer from predevelopment until the 1983–85 time-averaged model period (Hansen and others, 1994; Vaccaro, 1999). Nearly all of this increased storage occurred beneath the Columbia Basin Irrigation Project beginning in about 1950. The episodic increase in storage following the onset of surface-water irrigation in the 1950s had ceased by the 1980s (earlier in many places) because the former vadose zone was essentially fully saturated. The coincidental increase in water storage in the uppermost basalt aquifer beneath the same area was only 2.0 km^3 (Hansen and others, 1994; Vaccaro, 1999), indicating

that most of the increased recharge is balanced by increased discharge to agricultural drains, streams, and rivers. In the next deeper basalt aquifer, water-level changes were mixed, but declines generally prevailed over rises, yielding a net depletion of about 4.2 km^3 in these deeper units (J.J. Vaccaro, written commun., 2008). The net cumulative increase in storage during this period is therefore approximately 10.1 km^3.

Since the early 1980s, conditions in the overburden aquifer have remained relatively stable, while net water-level declines have dominated in the deeper units. Some water-level change maps are available (Snyder and Haynes, 2010). Groundwater levels measured in the spring of 1984 and 2009 in 470 wells were compared. Small to moderate groundwater-level declines were measured in most wells, although declines greater than 30 m and as great as 91 m were measured in many wells. Of the wells measured in 1984 and 2009, water levels declined in 83 percent of the wells, and declines greater than 7.6 m were measured in 29 percent of all wells. The groundwater-level changes were greatest in the deeper hydrogeologic units. To develop an approximate time history of depletion, generalizations about the rates of water-level changes will be used as a basis for extrapolation. It is assumed that the early water-level rises were negligible prior to 1950 and then continued at a uniform rate through 1965, when water-level rises were balanced by water-level declines. It is further assumed that this balance and stabilization of depletion continued through 1970, after which water-level declines dominated the system.

The model for the time-averaged period in the mid-1980s indicated an average storage reduction rate of 5.3 m^3/s (0.17 km^3/yr) (Hansen and others, 1994; Vaccaro, 1999). Recent linearly trending water-level declines indicate that this rate represents a conservative estimate for more recent storage loss. Assuming that this rate of storage depletion applies from 1971 through 2008, it is estimated that the net change in storage during this latter time period is about -6.5 km^3. Using these simplifying assumptions, an approximate history of cumulative changes in storage can be constructed (fig. 47). This plot indicates that during the 20th century about 5.2 km^3 of water has been added to subsurface storage, and by 2008 this had decreased to 3.8 km^3 (table 1). This represents a small increase in the estimated depletion relative to Konikow (2011). Although the net change in groundwater storage in the system since 1900 has been positive, it is reasonable to expect that the net change in storage will become a negative depletion in the future (by 2030 if calculated recent rates continue unchanged).

Oahu, Hawaii

The largest and most productive flow system on the island of Oahu, Hawaii, is the central Oahu flow system (figs. 1 and 2). Growth in population, agriculture, and the tourism industry has placed demands on the flow system since the beginning of development. The mild climate, with dry summers and wet winters, is primarily controlled by topography and persistent northeasterly trade winds. Sanderson

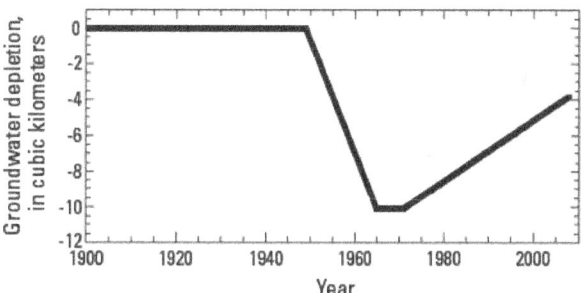

Figure 47. Cumulative groundwater depletion in the Columbia Plateau aquifer system, Washington, Oregon, and Idaho, 1900 through 2008.

(1993) and Oki (1998) provide more detailed descriptions of the hydrologic setting of Oahu.

Pliocene and Pleistocene volcanic rocks compose the principal aquifers for the island. Two major volcanoes formed Oahu with major rift zones radiating from their calderas. Groundwater generally flows from areas of high recharge near the mountainous interior parts of the island to areas of discharge near the coast. Low permeability is characteristic of weathered volcanic rocks and of the dike complexes found in the major rift zones. The occurrence of weathered deposits and dike complexes leads to a difference in water levels between adjacent regions. Water-table elevations can differ markedly on opposite sides of a dike, but water-table slopes are relatively gentle where the aquifer is continuous. High permeability is observed in the dike-free deposits (Oki and others, 1999). Coastal deposits, consisting of terrestrial and marine sediments and limestone reef deposits, form coastal plains in southern and northern Oahu (Oki, 1998). Hunt (1996) and Oki (1998) provide more detailed descriptions of the hydrogeology of Oahu.

The first well on the island of Oahu was drilled in 1879, and 86 wells had been drilled by 1890. Further rapid development occurred between 1891 and 1910 with the launch of irrigation of sugarcane. Over 1,184 wells, tunnels, and shafts had been constructed, with over 800 of the structures still in use, by the year 1985 (Nichols and others, 1996). Drainage into water-supply tunnels has caused substantial reductions of volumes of dike-impounded groundwater in storage, and the construction of eight tunnels in Oahu caused a depletion of about 0.1 km³ on the windward side of the island (Takasaki, 1978).

Few records on pumpage were kept before 1910, but water-level declines had been noted by this point. Heavy development of the aquifer system continued throughout the middle half of the century, primarily in the north-central and southern regions of the island, with expansion of sugarcane irrigation and population growth. Pumpage from the central Oahu flow system peaked in 1977 at an annual rate about 0.51 km³/yr and declined somewhat to a rate of about 0.27 km³/yr during the 12-month period prior to July 1995 (Oki, 1998). Data indicate that about 91 percent of the total freshwater

withdrawals from Oahu County were produced in the groundwater areas of the central Oahu flow system (Nichols and others, 1996). The total groundwater withdrawal volume during 1900–95 was about 31 km³. Mean annual groundwater withdrawal rates have been more or less stable during 1995–2008 (Rotzoll and others, 2010, fig. 3C).

Reported values of specific yield range from less than 0.01 to 0.19 (Hunt, 1996; Nichols and others, 1996). Oki (2005) developed a model of the Pearl Harbor area and used specific yield values of 0.20 for the upper limestone caprock unit, 0.04 for the volcanic-rock aquifer east of Waiawa Stream, and 0.10 for all other rocks. On this basis, it is simply assumed that a central value for specific yield of 0.10 is adequately representative for the purpose of estimating the volume of groundwater depletion.

Long-term changes in groundwater levels are presented for selected representative wells by Nichols and others (1996), Oki (1998), Oki and others (1999), Oki (2005), and Rotzoll and others (2010). These generally indicate a long-term trend of declining water levels during the period 1900–2003. Rotzoll and others (2010) report that relatively wet years probably caused water levels to rise between 2005 and 2007—representing a recovery of about 20 percent in the water levels in a monitoring well near Honolulu. The long-term declines varied from area to area, but they were generally in the range of 1 to 3 m in many areas, and largest in the heavily developed Honolulu area. Integrating these changes over the respective areas indicates a total depletion volume of about 0.12 km³. In constructing a history of depletion over time, it is assumed that the depletion from pumpage accumulates with a linear trend from 1900 to 2003, and that there is then a recovery of 20 percent from 2005 to 2007. It is also assumed that the reduction in storage related to tunnels accumulates uniformly during 1900–60, which includes the time during which most tunnels were constructed (Takasaki and others, 1969). The results (fig. 48; table 1) yield an estimate of total depletion of 0.22 km³ by 2000 and 0.20 km³ in 2008.

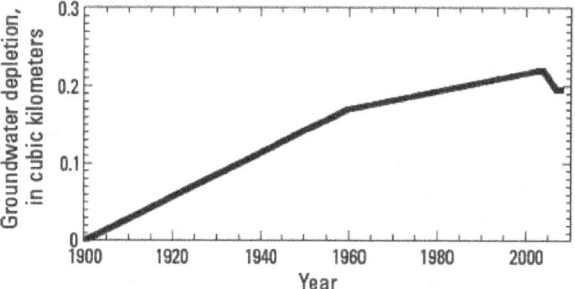

Figure 48. Cumulative groundwater depletion in Oahu, Hawaii, 1900 through 2008.

Snake River Plain, Idaho

The Snake River Plain aquifer system underlies the crescent-shaped lowland that extends from eastern Idaho to the

Idaho-Oregon border (figs. 1 and 2). The aquifer system is one the most productive systems in the United States (Orr, 1997). The Snake River Plain aquifer system consists of a thick sequence of volcanic rocks and covers an area of approximately 40,000 km² (Whitehead, 1994). The Snake River Plain has an arid climate, and the average annual precipitation over much of the plain is 20 to 25 cm. Runoff into the basin from the surrounding mountains and surface-water and groundwater discharge in the basin mostly drains into the Snake River (Kjelstrom, 1995).

The western Snake River Plain lies within a deep structural depression. Quaternary basalts are interbedded with sediments deposited by the Snake River and tributary streams along the margins of the eastern plain (Garabedian, 1992). The sedimentary interbeds are as much as 15 m thick and consist of well to poorly sorted clay, silt, sand, and gravel (Orr, 1997). The hydrogeology of the Snake River Plain is described in greater detail by Whitehead (1992); that of the western and eastern parts is described by Newton (1991) and Garabedian (1992), respectively.

The regional aquifer system is generally unconfined; however, local confined conditions are apparent in places (Garabedian, 1992). Substantial quantities of recharge to the aquifer system have been supplied from surface-water diversions used for irrigation. Water-level rises of as much as 60 m have been observed in the eastern plain since irrigation began. Other areas have made use of the groundwater resources of the aquifer system for irrigation—resulting in large water-level declines (Whitehead, 1994).

The history of irrigation and water use on the Snake River Plain through 1980 indicates there was little development of groundwater resources for irrigation in the western plain in the early 1900s (Goodell, 1988). Pumpage has increased steadily, however, since the late 1940s (Newton, 1991). Initial development of irrigation in the eastern plain began around 1880 with the Snake River as the source. A rapid increase in development occurred in 1895 when many diversions and canals had been constructed (Kjelstrom, 1995). Groundwater use for irrigation in the eastern plain increased substantially beginning in the late 1940s, but slowed by the 1970s when surface-water withdrawals from the Snake River increased significantly. By 1980, roughly 10,500 km² of the eastern plain were irrigated with 2.3 km³/yr of groundwater pumped from the eastern Snake River Plain aquifer system (Kjelstrom, 1995).

Groundwater levels in the western Snake River Plain aquifer system have changed considerably since the early 1900s. Some areas have experienced significant rises from irrigation recharge. One well in Ada County showed a rise of about 24 m since 1914; other areas, such as Elmore County, have shown declines of as much as 11 m since the 1960s (Newton, 1991). Groundwater levels in the eastern Snake River Plain aquifer system generally increased prior to the early 1950s because of the increased recharge from surface-water diversions. As groundwater use for irrigation increased, use of sprinkler irrigation systems occurred, and

several periods of below normal precipitation occurred. Water levels began an overall decline from the early 1950s to 1980 (Kjelstrom, 1995).

Annual groundwater budgets were calculated for the eastern Snake River Plain for 1912 to 1980 and for the western Snake River Plain for 1930 to 1980 (Kjelstrom, 1995). Cumulatively, the increase in groundwater storage from 1930 to 1980 in the western plain was estimated as 2.7 km³. Results of a groundwater model analysis (Newton, 1991) indicated that about 0.7 km³ was added to storage in the western plain from 1900 through 1930, so the total increase in storage in the western Snake River Plain is approximately 3.4 km³ during 1900–80. Groundwater storage increased in the main part of the eastern plain by 15.3 km³ from 1912 to 1980 and in the southern part of the eastern plain by 5.4 km³ in that same time period, for a total of 20.7 km³ added to storage in the eastern Snake River Plain. Storage increased by about 7.4 km³ from the start of irrigation (1880) through 1911 in the main part of the eastern plain and by 2.5 km³ in the southern part of the eastern plain (Kjelstrom, 1995). Assuming that half of that is attributable to the period 1900–11, the total change in groundwater storage in the eastern Snake River Plain from 1900 through 1980 is approximately 25.7 km³. Therefore, on the basis of a direct budget analysis, the total change in storage in the entire Snake River Plain during 1900–80 is an increase of approximately 29.1 km³.

A transient, 3D, groundwater-flow model of the western Snake River Plain aquifer system was developed (Newton, 1991) using the MODFLOW model (McDonald and Harbaugh, 1988). The transient model used nine 10-year stress periods to simulate long-term water-level changes from pre-irrigation time (1890) until 1980. The model grid included 25 rows and 72 columns of square cells 3.2 km on a side. The groundwater system was divided vertically into three layers. Other hydraulic properties, boundary conditions, and calibration methods are described in more detail by Newton (1991). The calibrated model computed a water budget for each stress period in the 90-year simulation. The net change in storage from 1900 until 1980 was estimated as an addition of 1.5 km³ in the western Snake River Plain aquifer system. The rate of increase in storage was the greatest during the period 1910–20, and generally decreased afterwards to a very small rate of 0.0026 km³/yr during the 1970s.

A transient, 3D, groundwater-flow model of the eastern Snake River Plain aquifer system was developed by Garabedian (1992). This model also used the MODFLOW model (McDonald and Harbaugh, 1988). The transient simulation represented the years 1891 to 1980 and was divided into eighteen 5-year stress periods. The finite-difference grid included 21 rows and 51 columns of square cells that were 4.6 km on a side. The system was vertically divided into four model layers. The model used spatially varying values of specific yield that ranged from 0.05 to 0.20 (Garabedian, 1992). For 1901–80, it was estimated that 59.3 km³ was added to storage in the eastern Snake River Plains aquifer system. The largest annual increases occurred between 1900 and 1925, but during the last 5 years of the analysis (1975–80), there was a decrease in the volume of groundwater in storage.

Combining the results of the two models (Newton, 1991; Garabedian, 1992) yields an estimate of the total cumulative net depletion of groundwater in the entire Snake River Plain from 1900 through 1980 of -60.8 km³—approximately twice that computed by the direct budget approach. Because there can be errors and uncertainty in both approaches, which cannot be easily resolved, it is assumed that a best estimate of the change in storage can be derived by averaging the annual values of the two approaches. This yields an increase in groundwater storage from 1900 through 1980 of 45.0 km³.

An enhanced Snake River Plain aquifer model was subsequently developed by Cosgrove and others (2006) to simulate the 22-year period from 1980 through 2002. Groundwater levels have generally declined in the central part of the plain from 1980 through 2002, and declines typically ranged from about 1.5 to 3 m (Cosgrove and others, 2006). This corresponds to an annual decrease in storage during 1980–2001 of approximately 0.18 km³/yr (Cosgrove and others, 2006).

The 1980 estimates are extended by assuming that there were no further changes in storage in the western Snake River Plain through 2008 and that the average rate of depletion from the newer enhanced model for the eastern Snake River Plain (Cosgrove and others, 2006) applies for the entire period of 1981 through 2008. This results in a total net increase in groundwater storage of 41.4 km³ by 2000 and 39.9 km³ by 2008 (fig. 49; table 1).

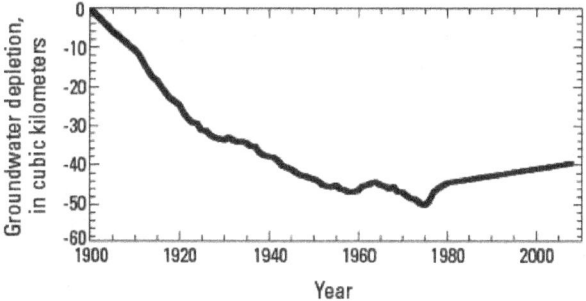

Figure 49.   Cumulative groundwater depletion in the Snake River Plain aquifer system, Idaho, 1900 through 2008.

Deep Confined Bedrock Aquifers

Black Mesa Area, Arizona

The Black Mesa area is a 14,000 km² arid to semiarid region in northeastern Arizona (figs. 1 and 2). Groundwater is the only source of water for municipal and industrial uses. The N-aquifer, or Navajo Aquifer, is the most important source of groundwater in the region. Rainfall in most outcrop areas is less than 30 cm/yr, and recharge represents only one to three percent of precipitation (Eychaner, 1983).

Prior to the mid 1960s, development of the N-aquifer system was minor and withdrawals were spread over such a large area that the aquifer was considered to remain in equilibrium; the aquifer system contained at least 220 km³ of water in storage (Eychaner, 1983). Substantial municipal and industrial development began in the early 1970s. Since then, large water-level declines have been observed in a number of wells. Through 2001, the median water-level change in 33 wells was -5.2 m, and water-level changes in 15 wells completed in unconfined aquifers ranged from -12 m to +1.9 m (Thomas, 2002).

The N-aquifer is a multiple-aquifer system. The principal lithologic unit is a sandstone that reaches a maximum saturated thickness of over 300 m in the northwestern part of the area. The 8,550-km² central part of the area is under confined conditions and the aquifer is unconfined to the east, north, and west of Black Mesa (Eychaner, 1983). Eychaner (1983) reports that the confined storage coefficient is 0.0004 where the aquifer is thickest, and the estimated specific yield ranges from 0.10 to 0.15.

Data on the historical groundwater withdrawals from the N-aquifer system indicate that municipal withdrawals began in 1965, and in 2001 there were over 70 wells in operation (Thomas, 2002). More than 0.038 km³ and 0.041 km³ of withdrawals were made from confined and unconfined aquifers, respectively, during 1965–2000. Industrial withdrawals started in 1968; most of this water was used to supply a coal slurry pipeline. From 1968 through 2000, roughly 0.14 km³ of groundwater from the N-aquifer system has been produced. The total groundwater withdrawals through 2000 were about 0.22 km³.

A two-dimensional groundwater-flow model was developed to predict the effects of withdrawals in the N-Aquifer (Eychaner, 1983). The model was calibrated for equilibrium (pre-1965) and nonequilibrium conditions through 1979 (Eychaner, 1983). The results indicated that about 95 percent of water pumped during 1965–79 was withdrawn from storage, although the reduction amounted to less than 0.03 percent of the total volume in storage.

The model was updated as monitoring of the region continued. Brown and Eychaner (1988) converted the original model to one based on the U.S. Geological Survey's MODFLOW model. The model was recalibrated using revised estimates of selected aquifer parameters, a finer spatial grid, withdrawal data from 1965 through 2001, and observed water-level changes through 2001 (Brown and Eychaner, 1988; Hart and Sottilare, 1988, 1989; Bills and Brown, 1992; Thomas, 2002).

The continued data collection allowed the model to simulate a 36-year period of record. The cumulative water budget computed by this model indicated a net change in storage through 2000 of approximately 0.22 km³. This depletion is equivalent to 93 percent of the total withdrawal, which is consistent with the earlier estimate (Eychaner, 1983). The depletion is estimated as 0.26 km³ for 2008 by extrapolating the rate of depletion during the last 9 years of the simulation through 2008 (fig. 50; table 1).

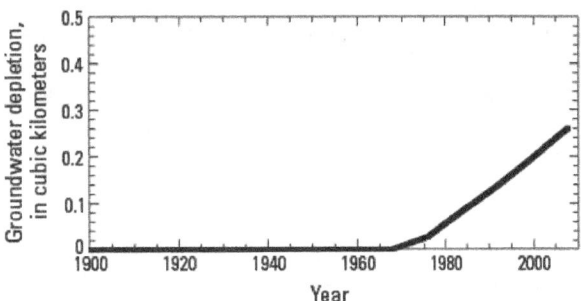

Figure 50.   Cumulative groundwater depletion in the Black Mesa area, Arizona, 1900 through 2008.

Midwest Cambrian-Ordovician Aquifer System

The Cambrian-Ordovician aquifer system extends over a 417,000 km^2 area in parts of Minnesota, Wisconsin, Iowa, Illinois, Indiana, Michigan, and Missouri (figs. 1 and 2). The aquifer system is a relatively continuous sequence of sandstone and carbonate rocks overlying Precambrian crystalline basement rock. It consists of alternating pairs of aquifers and overlying low-permeability confining units (Young, 1992a). The hydrogeology is described in more detail by Young (1992b) and Mandle and Kontis (1992). Groundwater supplied from the aquifer system is widely used by the region's many metropolitan areas for municipal and industrial supply. Withdrawals are also used for industrial, rural, and domestic supply (Young, 1992a). Surface drainage in the study area flows mainly to the Mississippi River and its major tributaries, such as the Missouri River. A small part of the study area lies within the Lake Michigan drainage basin (Young, 1992b). Average annual precipitation increases from 61 cm in the northwest to 112 cm in the southeast, averaging 81 cm over the study area.

Rapid development of the Cambrian-Ordovician aquifer system began in the late 1800s with the first deep well drilled in the Chicago area around 1864. Uncontrolled flow from flowing artesian wells and large withdrawals led to significant head declines by the early 1900s. The most significant head declines occurred in the confined aquifers around the metropolitan areas of Chicago, Illinois, Milwaukee and Green Bay, Wisconsin, and Mason City, Iowa (Young, 1992a). During 1976–80, withdrawals from wells in the Cambrian-Ordovician aquifer system in the entire study area averaged about 0.95 km^3/yr (Young, 1992a).

The deep, confined, Cambrian-Ordovician aquifer system became the most important system in the northern Illinois region with the population and industrial expansion in Chicago. A considerable number of wells had been drilled by the turn of the century and continued to increase at an irregular rate until the mid-1950s. After this time, a dramatic increase

in withdrawals was observed (Visocky, 1997) until withdrawals from the eight-county region surrounding the Chicago metropolitan area reached its maximum in 1979. Around 1980, fears of depleting the system led public water suppliers in the area to shift their source of water to Lake Michigan (Healy and others, 2007). Beginning in 1980, withdrawal rates declined for the first time since the early 1940s. By then, heads had declined as much as 300 m in places (Young, 1992a). Recovery of water levels have been observed in some areas of the northern Illinois region as a result of the surface-water diversions and reduced withdrawals, though substantial residual drawdowns persisted (for example, see Healy and others, 2007, fig. 52). But water-level declines progressed further in other areas associated with continued heavy withdrawals. For example, from 1975 to 1997, water levels in the Cambrian-Ordovician aquifer system declined in large areas in central and eastern Iowa—by as much as 40 m (Turco, 1999, fig. 5). In northeastern Illinois, water levels recovered rapidly during the early 1980s and became generally stable in the 1990s. However, Burch (2008) reports that declining water levels returned after 2000, with declines in the 8 to 15 m range during 2000–2007. In southeastern Wisconsin, a number of deep observation wells show long-term steady declines in water levels from the 1940s through 2000 (Feinstein and others, 2004).

A quasi-three-dimensional groundwater-flow model of the aquifer system was developed by Mandle and Kontis (1992) using the code from Trescott and Larson (1976). However, the modeled area excluded that part of the aquifer system in Michigan. The aquifers were represented by five model layers, and intervening confining layers were not explicitly simulated, so changes in storage in confining layers are not computed. The spatial grid includes 40 columns and 37 rows of square cells that are approximately 27.7 km on a side. More detailed information on the hydraulic properties, boundary and initial conditions, and calibration approach are presented by Mandle and Kontis (1992). An initial steady-state simulation was calibrated to represent predevelopment conditions prior to 1861 and to provide consistent initial conditions for the transient simulation, which represented the period 1861–1980 in 12 stress periods. In the final 5-year stress period (1976–80), the total pumpage averaged 34.2 m^3/s and the release from aquifer storage averaged 6.1 m^3/s (or 0.96 km^3 during the stress period—about 18 percent of the pumpage). The model results indicated that during 1900–80, there was a total of 7.2 km^3 of depletion from storage in aquifers.

Because the model did not simulate storage changes in confining units, that was estimated using the method of Konikow and Neuzil (2007). The method was applied separately to the parts of the aquifer system in the five separate States in which it occurs. The assumed value for specific storage of the uppermost confining unit, the Maquoketa shale, was based on the model value of 1.1×10^{-6} m^{-1} used by Eaton and others (2000, fig. 4). Breemer and others (2002) assigned a value of $S_S = 4.6 \times 10^{-6}$ m^{-1} to all layers in a transient flow model applied to a generally north-south flowline extending through most of Illinois, and this value was assumed applicable to the two deeper confining units, the St. Lawrence-Franconia and the Eau Claire confining units. These values were assumed to be constant in space. Average values of vertical hydraulic conductivity for each confining unit in each State were estimated from values presented by Young (1992b). Average values of the long-term (predevelopment to 1980) head change in each aquifer were estimated from model calculations of Mandle and Kontis (1992, figs. 34A–C). This analysis indicates that an additional depletion of about 4.2 km³ is attributable to reduced storage in the confining units adjacent to the aquifers of the Cambrian-Ordovician aquifer system through 1980. This includes about 3.2 km³ in Illinois, 0.62 km³ in Iowa, 0.0 km³ in Minnesota, 0.01 km³ in Missouri, and 0.34 km³ in Wisconsin. In 1980, this represented about 56 percent of the depletion from aquifers, and it is assumed that this same ratio applies for all years.

To extrapolate the record from 1981 through 2008, it is assumed that during 1981–99 the recovery in northeastern Illinois completely offsets additional depletion in other areas, but from 2000 through 2008, depletion continues at half the average rate computed for the last 5 years of the model study. These assumptions led to a total cumulative depletion in 2000 of 11.4 km³ and in 2008 of 12.6 km³ (fig. 51; table 1). This estimate is slightly less than that published in Konikow (2011) because the estimates for depletion from confining units (described above) have been refined since the original analysis.

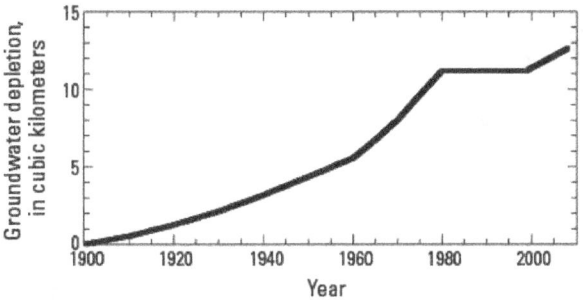

Figure 51. Cumulative groundwater depletion in the Cambrian-Ordovician aquifer system, Minnesota, Wisconsin, Iowa, Illinois, and Missouri, 1900 through 2008.

Dakota Aquifer, Northern Great Plains

The Dakota and related sandstones in west-central North America comprise an extensive aquifer (Konikow and Neuzil, 2007) (figs. 1 and 2). The Dakota aquifer is considered a classic example of an artesian aquifer system. This large aquifer system is extensively developed in South Dakota, where it underlies more than 171,000 km² (LeRoux and Hamilton, 1985). It also occurs in several adjacent States (Jorgensen and Signor, 1984). Study of the aquifer system began around the

turn of the 20th century (for example, see Darton, 1896, 1905, 1909), and helped shape current ideas about artesian aquifers (Bredehoeft and others, 1983).

Substantial development of the aquifer system in South Dakota had begun by the early 1880s (Bredehoeft and others, 1983). By 1905, over 1,000 wells (including many flowing wells) were producing water in the State east of the Missouri River, supplying an estimated 1.2×10⁶ m³/d of water for irrigation and livestock (Bredehoeft and others, 1983). Estimated withdrawals stabilized at about 150,000 m³/d by 1960 (Helgesen and others, 1984). Large rates of head decline in the Dakota aquifer occurred before 1915. Pumpage data (Bredehoeft and others, 1983; Case, 1984; Helgesen and others, 1984) indicate that the cumulative well discharge from the Dakota aquifer system in South Dakota from predevelopment in the early 1880s to 1981 totaled about 19.7 km³ of water. During the 20th century, the total withdrawals were approximately 17.8 km³.

Groundwater depletion from the Dakota aquifer system in South Dakota was evaluated using potentiometric maps showing predevelopment (Darton, 1909) and 1980 conditions (Case, 1984). Estimates of dimensionless storage coefficient values for the Dakota aquifer range from 1.0×10⁻⁴ to 1.0×10⁻⁵ (Bredehoeft and others, 1983); a central value of 5.0×10⁻⁵ was used to estimate depletion in this confined aquifer system. Integrating the head change over the study area, and accounting for the confined storage properties, indicates that a total of about 0.4 km³ of groundwater was derived from storage in the aquifer for the period from predevelopment through 1980.

Since development, most of the water released from storage originated from the confining layers (Bredehoeft and others, 1983). A model-calibration estimate for the value of specific storage was 1.6×10⁴ m⁻¹, and this was assumed to be a representative value for all confining units (Bredehoeft and others, 1983). The total calculated volume of water removed from storage from confining units in South Dakota up to 1980 was thereby estimated at 14.9 ±2.2 km³ (Konikow and Neuzil, 2007).

The total depletion in South Dakota during 1880–1980 is thus about 15.3 km³. This represents about 78 percent of the total withdrawals. Applying this same ratio to the 20th century withdrawals indicates that depletion during 1900–2000 was approximately 13.9 km³. Extrapolation for eight additional years at the 1995–2000 rate indicates that the total depletion by 2008 is about 14.4 km³.

Although the Dakota aquifer is developed in several States in addition to South Dakota, data on long-term withdrawals and water-level declines are sparse—in part because the aquifer is very deep in some of the areas. Some data are available for the Dakota aquifer in parts of Kansas, Iowa, Nebraska, and Colorado (Jorgensen and Signor, 1984), and estimates are made of long-term depletion in these States (recognizing that the aquifer system is even more extensive than this). In the Denver Basin of Colorado, the Dakota is deep and is confined by thick low-permeability confining units, so the analyses of the Denver Basin aquifer system excludes the Dakota (see Paschke and others, 2011b). Estimates of total cumulative depletion for 1900–2000 (table 3) are based on estimates of aquifer and confining unit properties and approximations of long-term changes in head in the aquifer and adjacent confining units (using the method of Konikow and Neuzil, 2007) and have been updated since the estimates of Konikow (2011). Hence, the estimated values of depletion in table 3 are slightly greater than those previous estimates. The estimates in table 3 have a greater uncertainty associated with them than the estimate for the Dakota in South Dakota and indicate additional depletion volumes of 0.1 km³ (Iowa), 0.8 km³ (Colorado), 2.5 km³ (Kansas), and 2.3 km³ (Nebraska). It is further assumed that the total depletion of about 5.7 km³ in these four States during 1900–2000 grew proportionately to that in South Dakota, where more data are available. This results in a total depletion for the Dakota aquifer system in these five States of about 20.1 km³ during 1900–2000 and 20.3 km³ through 2008 (fig. 52; table 1).

Table 3.   Estimated groundwater depletion in the Dakota aquifer system and adjacent confining units in Colorado, Iowa, Kansas, and Nebraska (1900–2000).

[km³, cubic kilometer]

	Aquifer (km³)	Confining unit (km³)	Total (km³)
Colorado	0.2	0.6	0.8
Iowa	0.04	0.1	0.1
Kansas	0.7	1.8	2.5
Nebraska	0.3	2.0	2.3
Total	1.2	4.5	5.7

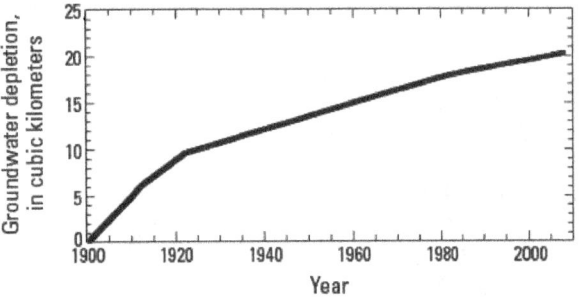

Figure 52.   Cumulative groundwater depletion in the Dakota aquifer system, South Dakota, Colorado, Iowa, Kansas, and Nebraska, 1900 through 2008.

Denver Basin, Colorado

The Denver Basin bedrock aquifer system is an important source of water for municipal and agricultural purposes in the Denver and Colorado Springs areas of Colorado (Moore

and others, 2004) (figs. 1 and 2). The confined aquifer system consists of sedimentary rocks that comprise a series of aquifers and confining units, and an alluvial aquifer that overlies the bedrock system (Robson, 1989; Paschke and others, 2011b). The Denver Basin includes an area of about 18,000 km². The area has a semiarid continental climate, with 28 to 46 cm of average annual precipitation (Robson, 1989).

Groundwater development began in the 1880s with the completion of flowing artesian wells in Denver. The number of bedrock wells has increased from 12,000 in 1985 to 33,700 in 2001, and the withdrawal of groundwater has caused water-level declines of over 75 m (Moore and others, 2004). Total withdrawals increased notably starting in the 1930s (fig. 53). The vast majority of pumping from the alluvial aquifer is for irrigation use; municipal usage is the largest of the bedrock pumpage (Paschke and others, 2011a). A detailed description of the history of groundwater development and use in the area is presented by Paschke and others (2011a).

A 3D transient groundwater-flow model of the basin was developed and calibrated by Banta and others (2011) using MODFLOW-2000 (Harbaugh and others, 2000). A steady-state model was calibrated first to represent predevelopment conditions prior to 1880. Then a 124-year transient model was calibrated to represent conditions from 1880 through 2003 using 15 model stress periods ranging from 2 to 27 years in length. The model grid has 84 columns and 124 rows of square cells; each cell measures 1.6 km by 1.6 km. The system was discretized vertically into 12 model layers to represent seven aquifers and five confining units, with the uppermost model layer representing the unconfined alluvial aquifer (Banta and others, 2011). The model assumptions, parameters, boundary conditions, and calibration process are described in detail by Banta and others (2011).

The model results included calculated changes in storage since predevelopment time. They show increased rates of depletion from the bedrock aquifers since the 1970s, but these are partly offset by substantial increases in storage in the unconfined alluvial aquifers since the late 1980s. Considering both the unconfined and confined aquifers, the total net model-calculated cumulative depletion in the Denver Basin in 2003 was 1.00 km³. During the last 4 years of the simulation, the average rate of depletion was 0.059 km³/yr. Depletion is extrapolated to 2008, assuming this rate applies during 2004–08. The total groundwater depletion from 1900 through 2000 is 0.82 km³ and from 1900 through 2008 is 1.30 km³ (fig. 54; table 1).

Agricultural and Land Drainage in the United States

During the 20th century, many agricultural and civil engineering projects were completed for land reclamation, flood control, and agricultural drainage purposes in the United States. This led to significant losses of wetland areas throughout the Nation. On farms, crop yields can be increased by

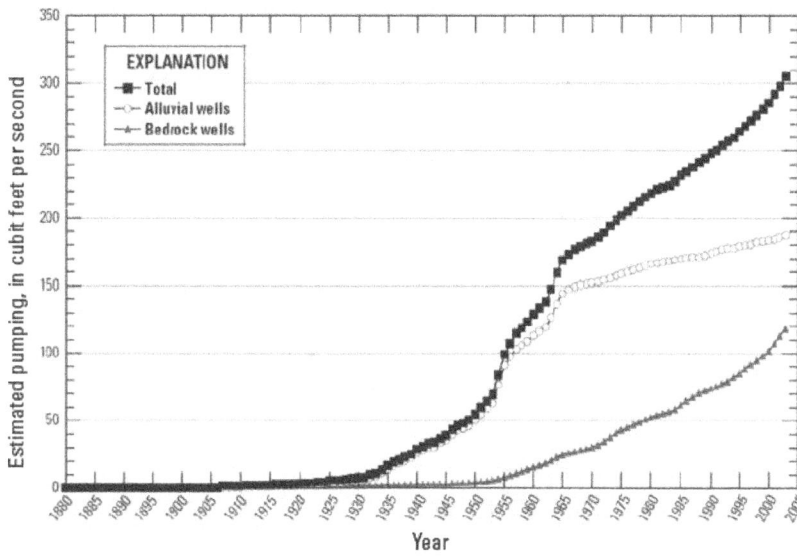

Figure 53. Total estimated pumping in the Denver Basin, Colorado, 1880 through 2003 (from Paschke and others, 2011a).

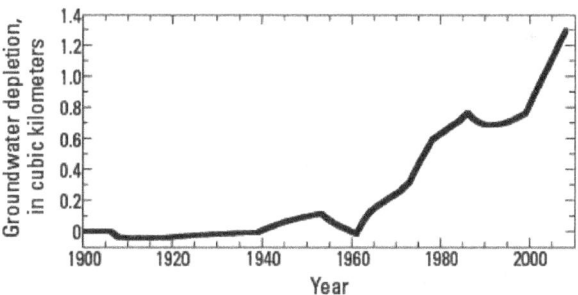

Figure 54. Cumulative groundwater depletion in the Denver Basin, Colorado, 1900 through 2008.

keeping the water table some distance below the land surface, thereby precluding waterlogging of land and allowing salts to be removed from the soil profile. Drainage projects can result in permanently lowered water-table elevations both locally and regionally. Where the seasonal or average annual position of the water table is permanently lowered, the net decline represents a long-term depletion of the volume of groundwater in storage below the land surface.

The first half of the 20th century was marked by emerging technologies for land drainage. Farmers joined together in drainage organizations to build drainage and flood control measures. Large-scale drainage projects backed by drainage organizations and Federal agencies affected both large and small wetland areas. Agricultural and urban expansion persisted throughout the United States. Use of drained lands usually occurred in a succession, from undrained wetlands to agricultural lands to urban areas. These factors led to the drainage of many tens of thousands of square kilometers in the conterminous United States during the 20th century.

There are two approaches for land drainage surveys. The first is to catalogue drained lands. The Bureau of the Census reported a regular Census of Drainage Organizations between 1920 and 1978. The data were compiled and averaged on a county-wide basis by the local Soil Conservation Service (Pavelis, 1987). More than 433,000 km[2] of farmland were being drained in 1985.

The second approach for calculating the drained area in the United States is to compare the area of wetlands remaining in the year 2000 to the extent of wetlands in 1900. Two Federal agencies maintain inventories of wetland areas. The U.S. Fish and Wildlife Service collects data every 10 years for their Status and Trends database (for example, see Dahl, 1990, 2000). The U.S. Department of Agriculture's National Resources Conservation Service uses soil surveys to adjust their National Resources Inventory on a 5-year cycle (Heimlich and others, 1998). For this analysis, a calibration between the two inventories leads to a single inventory containing an estimate of the areal extent of wetlands in the conterminous United States. The adjusted inventory indicates that approximately 720,000 km[2] of wetlands were distributed throughout the country in the year 1900. The most recent year available for the calibrated dataset was 1992, and the total area of wetlands remaining for that year was 459,000 km[2].

To estimate depletion associated with the drainage that is coincident with the loss of wetlands, it is assumed that drainage and loss of wetlands lowered the water table from at or near land surface to a generally optimal water-table depth for crops of about 1.06 m below ground level (Roe and Ayers, 1954). The loss in wetlands for these 92 years is approximately 261,000 km[2]. If this entire area were drained uniformly to the assumed optimal depth below the ground surface, and assuming an average porosity of 20 percent in these drained soils, then a volume of approximately 55 km[3] of water has been depleted from the subsurface more or less permanently (table 1).

While the drainage of wetlands in the United States has persisted throughout the century, the rate of loss had decreased markedly during the 1980s. Therefore, it is assumed that there is no additional wetland loss from 1992 to 2008 and that the historical rate of groundwater depletion caused by drainage is proportional to the percentage loss of wetlands during the 20th century, most of which occurred prior to 1950. The depletion volume in 2000 and 2008 would thus be the same as in 1992, when it was approximately 55 km³ (fig. 55). This is a small change (of 1 km³) from the value of Konikow (2011).

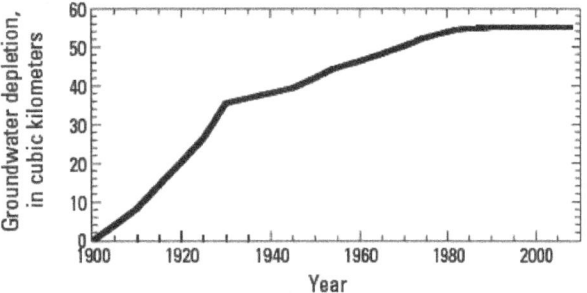

Figure 55. Cumulative groundwater depletion in the United States attributable to agricultural and land drainage projects, 1900 through 2008.

Discussion of Results

The 41 separate assessments (table 1) provide evidence that the long-term (1900–2008) cumulative depletion of groundwater in the United States is about 1,000 km³—about twice that of the volume of water contained in Lake Erie (about 480 km³). The depletion volume had increased from about 800 km³ in 2000—an increase of 25 percent in just 8 years. This large volume of depletion represents a serious problem in the United States because much of this storage loss cannot be easily or quickly recovered and affects the sustainability of some critical water supplies and base flow to streams, among other effects. The individual depletion assessments can be lumped into broader categories to help illustrate the magnitude of the problem (fig. 56). The three individual

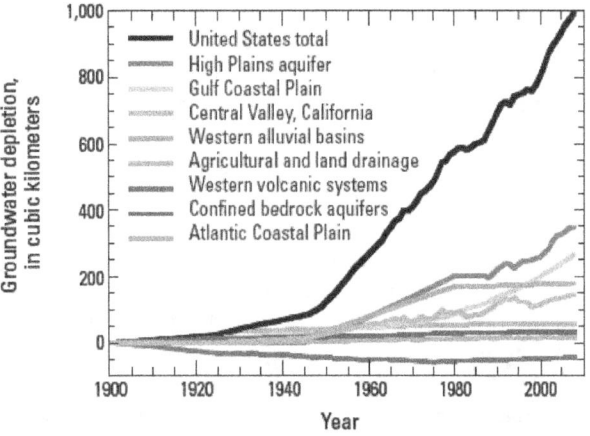

Figure 56. Cumulative groundwater depletion in the United States and major aquifer systems or categories, 1900 through 2008 (modified from Konikow, 2011).

systems that represent the largest contributors to groundwater depletion in the United States from 1900 through 2008 are principal aquifers—the High Plains aquifer (340.9 km³), the Mississippi embayment aquifer system (182.0 km³), and the Central Valley aquifer system of California (144.8 km³) (table 1).

The annual depletion volumes (fig. 56) can be used to estimate changes in the rate of depletion (fig. 57). The data shown in figure 57 represent averages over 10-year periods, except for the last period, which is averaged over the final 8 years of record. Annual rates of total groundwater depletion in the United States through 1945 were less than 4 km³/yr, but then increased substantially after the mid-1940s. The greatest rates of depletion occurred during 2001–2002 inclusive, when annual depletion rates averaged 34.8 km³/yr. Depletion rates during all of this most recent 8-year period averaged 23.9 km³/yr.

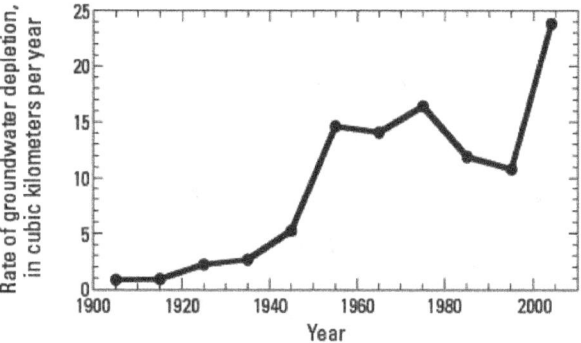

Figure 57. Decadal scale rate of groundwater depletion in the United States, 1900 through 2008. Final value represents average rate during an 8-year period, 2001 through 2008.

In addition to widely recognized adverse environmental effects of groundwater depletion, the depletion also impacts communities dependent on groundwater resources in that the continuation of depletion at observed rates makes the water supply unsustainable in the long term. However, depletion itself must certainly be unsustainable and the observed rates of depletion must eventually decrease as economic and physical constraints lead to reduced levels of extraction. Yet the data in table 2 and figure 57 demonstrate that the rates of depletion for some of the major aquifer system and land use categories during 2001–2008 are the highest since 1900, and in fact account for 25 percent of the total depletion during the 108-year period. Nevertheless, the rate of depletion is leveling off or becoming self-limiting in a number of areas, most notably the western alluvial basins (since 1980) and to a lesser degree the Central Valley (since the early 1990s).

Konikow (2011) also notes that oceans represent the ultimate sink for essentially all depleted groundwater. The surface area of the oceans is approximately 3.61×10^8 km² (Duxbury and others, 2000). If the estimated volumes of depletion were spread across the surface of the oceans, it would account for approximately 2.2 mm of sea-level rise from 1900 through 2000 and 2.8 mm of sea-level rise from 1900 through 2008. The observed rate of sea-level rise during the 20th century averaged about 1.7 mm/yr, but had increased to about 3.1 mm/yr since 2000 (Bindorf and others, 2007). Thus, depletion in the United States alone can explain 1.3 percent of the sea-level rise observed during the 20th century, and 2.3 percent of the observed rate of sea-level rise during 2001–2008.

All of the quantitative calculations underlying the estimates of groundwater depletion are based on limited observed data and assumptions and parameter values that contain uncertainties. Hence, all estimates should be revised and updated if new information becomes available. Furthermore, some areas may have experienced notable depletion that has not been included in this study, and if these depletions are recognized and quantified, they should be added to the total.

Conclusions

This study assessed long-term groundwater depletion in 40 separate aquifer systems or subareas, and one land use category. The cumulative volume of groundwater depletion in the United States during the 20th century is large—totaling about 800 cubic kilometers (km³) and increasing by an additional 25 percent during 2001–2008 (to a total volume of approximately 1,000 km³). Cumulative total groundwater depletion in the United States accelerated in the late 1940s and continued at an almost steady linear rate through the end of the century. In addition to widely recognized environmental consequences, groundwater depletion also adversely impacts the long-term sustainability of groundwater supplies to help meet the Nation's water needs. Groundwater depletion also is a small contributor to global sea-level rise, but sufficiently large that it needs to be recognized as a contributing factor and accounted for when explaining long-term global sea-level rise.

In general, unconfined aquifers exhibit greater volumetric depletion than do confined aquifers, although the latter tend to have greater water-level declines. Depletion in confined aquifers is derived primarily from leakage and storage depletion in adjacent low-permeability confining units. Depletion is also greater in the semiarid to arid western States than in the humid eastern States because of the greater potential for recharge to offset or balance withdrawals in humid areas.

A variety of methods were used to estimate long-term depletion in this study. The most reliable depend on direct measurements of water-level changes in the aquifer systems. In a few cases, independent methods were available to facilitate cross-checking of the accuracy of the estimates. These generally supported the reliability of the estimates.

References Cited

Abeyta, C.G., and Thomas, C.L., 1996, Hydrogeology and ground-water quality of the chromic acid pit site, U.S. Army Air Defense Artillery Center and Fort Bliss, El Paso, Texas: U.S. Geological Survey Water-Resources Investigations Report 96–4035, 67 p.

Alley, W.M., Reilly, T.E., and Franke, O.L., 1999, Sustainability of ground-water resources: U.S. Geological Survey Circular 1186, 79 p.

Anderson, T.W., 1995, Summary of the Southwest Alluvial Basins, Regional Aquifer-System Analysis, south-central Arizona and parts of adjacent states: U.S. Geological Survey Professional Paper 1406–A, 33 p.

Anderson, T.W., Freethey, G.W., and Tucci, Patrick, 1992, Geohydrology and water resources of alluvial basins in south-central Arizona and parts of adjacent states: U.S. Geological Survey Professional Paper 1406–B, 67 p.

Armstrong, C.A., and McMillion, L.G., 1961, Geology and ground-water resources of Pecos County, Texas: Texas Board of Water Engineers Bulletin 6106, v. 1, 435 p.

Ashworth, J.B., 1990, Evaluation of ground-water resources in parts of Loving, Pecos, Reeves, Ward, and Winkler Counties, Texas: Texas Water Development Board Report 317, 51 p.

Ator, S.W., Denver, J.M., Krantz, D.E., Newell, W.L., and Martucci, S.K., 2005, A surficial hydrogeologic framework for the Mid-Atlantic Coastal Plain: U.S. Geological Survey Professional Paper 1680, 44 p.

Aucott, W.R., 1996, Hydrology of the southeastern Coastal Plain aquifer system in South Carolina and parts of Georgia and North Carolina: U.S. Geological Survey Professional Paper 1410–E, 83 p.

Aucott, W.R., and Speiran, G.K., 1985, Ground-water flow in the Coastal Plain aquifers of South Carolina: Ground Water, v. 23, no. 6, p. 736–745.

Baker, E.T., Jr., 1979, Stratigraphic and hydrogeologic framework of part of the Coastal Plain of Texas: Texas Department of Water Resources Report 236, 43 p.

Baker, E.T., Jr., 1986, Hydrology of the Jasper aquifer in the southeast Texas Coastal Plain: Texas Water Development Board Report 295, 64 p.

Balleau Groundwater, Inc., 2009, Groundwater recharge analysis and estimate of recharge option costs: Town of Silver City, NM, Oct. 15, 2009, 55 p., Technical Memorandum accessed _February 24, 2012, at *http://www.townofsilvercity. org/utilities/Reprints/2009_11_03_Draft%20Balleau%20 Groundwater%20Recharge%20Analysis.pdf.*

Banta, E.R., Paschke, S.S., and Litke, D.W., 2011, Ground-water flow simulation of the Denver Basin aquifer system, Colorado, *in* Paschke, S.S., ed., Groundwater availability of the Denver Basin aquifer system, Colorado: U.S. Geological Survey Professional Paper 1770, chap. C, p. 181–274.

Barlow, P.M., 2003, Ground water in freshwater-saltwater environments of the Atlantic Coast: U.S. Geological Survey Circular 1262, 113 p.

Bartolino, J.R., and Cole, J.C., 2002, Ground-water resources of the Middle Rio Grande Basin, New Mexico: U.S. Geological Survey Circular 1222, 132 p.

Bartolino, J.R., and Cunningham, W.L., 2003, Ground-water depletion across the nation: U.S. Geological Survey Fact Sheet 103–03, 4 p.

Belcher, W.R., D'Agnese, F.A., and O'Brien, G.M., 2010, Introduction, *in* Belcher, W.R., and Sweetkind, D.S., eds., Death Valley regional groundwater flow system, Nevada and California—Hydrogeologic framework and transient groundwater flow model: U.S. Geological Survey Professional Paper 1711, chap. A, 17 p.

Belcher, W.R., Faunt, C.C., and D'Agnese, F.A., 2002, Three-dimensional hydrogeologic framework model for use with a steady-state numerical ground-water flow model of the Death Valley regional flow system, Nevada and California: U.S. Geological Survey Water-Resources Investigations Report 01–4254, 87 p.

Bell, J.W., 1981, Subsidence in Las Vegas Valley: Nevada Bureau of Mines and Geology Bulletin 95, 84 p.

Bertoldi, G.L., 1989, Ground-water resources of the Central Valley of California: U.S. Geological Survey Open-File Report 89–251, 2 p.

Bertoldi, G.L., Johnston, R.H., and Evenson, K.D., 1991, Ground water in the Central Valley, California—A summary report: U.S. Geological Survey Professional Paper 1401–A, 44 p.

Bexfield, L.M., and Anderholm, S.K., 2000, Predevelopment water-level map of the Santa Fe Group aquifer system in the Middle Rio Grande Basin between Cochiti Lake and San Acacia, New Mexico: U.S. Geological Survey Water-Resources Investigations Report 00–4249, 1 map sheet with text, scale approximately 1:400,000.

Bills, D.J., and Brown, J.G., 1992, Simulation of effects of pumping: *in* Sottilare, J.P., Results of ground-water, surface-water, and water-quality monitoring, Black Mesa area, northeastern Arizona—1989–90, U.S. Geological Survey Water-Resources Investigations Report 92–4008, p. 25–35.

Bindoff, N.L., Willebrand, Jürgen, Artale, Vincenzo, Cazenave, Anny, Gregory, J.M., Gulev, Sergey, Hanawa, Kimio, Le Quéré, Corrine, Levitus, Sydney, Nojiri, Yukihiro, Shum, C.K., Talley, L.D., and Unnikrishnan, A.S., 2007, Observations—Oceanic climate change and sea level, *in* Climate Change 2007—The physical science basis; Contribution of Working Group I to the Fourth Assessment Report of the Intergovernmental Panel on Climate Change, edited by S. Solomon, D. Qin, M. Manning, Z. Chen, M. Marquis, K.B. Averyt, M. Tignor, and H.L. Miller, Cambridge, U.K., Cambridge University Press, p. 385–432.

Boghici, Radu, 1999, Changes in groundwater conditions in parts of Trans-Pecos Texas, 1988–1998: Texas Water Development Board Report 348, 29 p.

Boghici, Radu, 2008, Changes in water levels in Texas, 1990 to 2000: Texas Water Development Board, Report 371, 34 p.

Bredehoeft, J.D., Neuzil, C.E., and Milly, P.C.D., 1983, Regional flow in the Dakota aquifer; a study of the role of confining layers: U.S. Geological Survey Water-Supply Paper 2237, 45 p.

Breemer, C.W., Clark, P.U., and Haggerty, Roy, 2002, Modeling the subglacial hydrology of the late Pleistocene Lake Michigan Lobe, Laurentide Ice Sheet: GSA Bulletin, v. 114, no. 6, p. 665–674.

Brown, J.G., and Eychaner, J.H., 1988, Simulation of five ground-water withdrawal projections for the Black Mesa area, Navajo and Hopi Indian Reservations, Arizona: U.S. Geological Survey Water-Resources Investigations Report 88–4000, 51 p.

Burbach, M.E., 2007, Groundwater-level changes in Nebraska from predevelopment to spring 2007: University of Nebraska–Lincoln, School of Natural Resources, Conservation and Survey data, accessed October 2008 at *http://snr5. unl.edu/csd-esic/GWMapArchives/2007GWMaps/Pred-2007.jpg*.

Burbey, T.J., 1995, Pumpage and water-level change in the principal aquifer of Las Vegas Valley, 1980–90: Nevada Division of Water Resources Information Report 34, 224 p.

Burch, S.L., 2008, A comparison of potentiometric surfaces for the Cambrian-Ordovician aquifers of northeastern Illinois, 2000 and 2007: Illinois State Water Survey Data/Case Study 2008–04, Champaign, Ill., 41 p.

Burns, E.R., Morgan, D.S., Peavler, R.S., and Kahle, S.C., 2011, Three-dimensional model of the geologic framework for the Columbia Plateau Regional Aquifer System, Idaho, Oregon, and Washington: U.S. Geological Survey Scientific Investigations Report 2010–5246, 44 p.

Busciolano, Ronald, 2005, Statistical analysis of long-term hydrologic records for selection of drought-monitoring sites on Long Island, New York: U.S. Geological Survey Scientific Investigations Report 2004–5152, 14 p.

Buxton, H.T., and Shernoff, P.K., 1999, Ground-water resources of Kings and Queens Counties, Long Island, New York: U.S. Geological Survey Water-Supply Paper 2498, 113 p., 7 pls.

Buxton, H.T., and Smolensky, D.A., 1999, Simulation of the effects of development of the ground-water flow system of Long Island, New York: U.S. Geological Survey Water-Resources Investigations Report 98–4069, 57 p.

Campbell, B.G., Fine, J.M., Petkewich, M.D., Coes, A.L., and Terziotti, Silvia, 2010, Chapter A—Groundwater availability in the Atlantic Coastal Plain of North and South Carolina, *in* Campbell, B.G., and Coes, A.L., eds., Groundwater availability in the Atlantic Coastal Plain of North and South Carolina: U.S. Geological Survey Professional Paper 1773, p. 1–47.

Carr, J.E., Meyer, W.R., Sandeen, W.M., and McLane, I.R., 1985, Digital models for simulation of groundwater hydrology of the Chicot and Evangeline aquifers along the Gulf Coast of Texas: Texas Department of Water Resources Report 289, 101 p.

Cartwright, R.A., 2002, History and hydrologic effects of ground-water use in Kings, Queens, and western Nassau Counties, Long Island, New York, 1800's through 1997: U.S. Geological Survey Water-Resources Investigations Report 01–4096, 79 p.

Case, H.L., 1984, Hydrogeology of the Inyan Kara and Dakota-Newcastle aquifer system, South Dakota, *in* Jorgensen, D.G. and Signor, D.C., eds., Geohydrology of the Dakota aquifer—Proceedings of the First C.V. Theis Conference on Geohydrology: Worthington, Ohio, National Water Well Association, p. 147–165.

Chowdhury, A.H., Wade, S., Mace, R.E., and Ridgeway, C., 2004, Groundwater availability model of the central Gulf Coast aquifer system—Numerical simulations through 1999: Texas Water Development Board Report, 90 p.

Christiansen, H.K., 2002, Escalante Valley, Beryl-Enterprise Area, *in* Ground-water conditions in Utah, Spring 2002, by C.B. Burden and others: Utah Division of Water Resources Cooperative Investigations Report No. 43, 120 p.

Clark, B.R., and Hart, R.M., 2009, The Mississippi Embayment Regional Aquifer Study (MERAS)—Documentation of a groundwater-flow model constructed to assess water availability in the Mississippi embayment: U.S. Geological Survey Scientific Investigations Report 2009–5172, 61 p.

Clarke, J.S., and Krause, R.E., 2000, Design, revision, and application of ground-water flow models for simulation of selected water-management scenarios in the coastal area of Georgia and adjacent parts of South Carolina and Florida: U.S. Geological Survey Water-Resources Investigations Report 00–4084, 93 p.

Cline, D.R., and Collins, C.A., 1992, Ground-water pumpage from the Columbia Plateau, Washington and Oregon, 1945 to 1984: U.S. Geological Survey Water-Resources Investigations Report 90–4085, 31 p.

Coes, A.L., Campbell, B.G., Petkewich, M.D., and Fine, J.M., 2010, Chapter C—Simulation of groundwater flow in the Atlantic Coastal Plain, North and South Carolina and parts of eastern Georgia and southern Virginia, Predevelopment to 2004, *in* Campbell, B.G., and Coes, A.L., eds., Groundwater availability in the Atlantic Coastal Plain of North and South Carolina: U.S. Geological Survey Professional Paper 1773, p. 163–241.

Cosgrove, D.M., Contor, B.A., and Johnson, G.S., 2006, Enhanced Snake Plain aquifer model final report: Idaho Water Resources Research Institute, University of Idaho, Technical Report 06–002, 120 p.

Dahl, T.E., 1990, Wetlands losses in the United States 1780s to 1980s: Washington, D.C., U.S. Fish and Wildlife Service, 58 p.

Dahl, T.E., 2000, Status and trends of wetlands in the conterminous United States 1986 to 1997: Washington, D.C., U.S. Fish and Wildlife Service, 82 p.

Darton, N.H., 1896, Preliminary report on artesian waters of a portion of the Dakotas: U.S. Geological Survey Annual Report, no. 17, pt. 2, p. 609-691.

Darton, N.H., 1905, Preliminary report on the geology and underground water resources of the central Great Plains: U.S. Geological Survey Professional Paper 32, 433 p.

Darton, N.H., 1909, Geology and underground waters of South Dakota: U.S. Geological Survey Water-Supply Paper 227, 156 p.

Dennehy, K.F., Litke, D.W., and McMahon, P.B., 2002, The High Plains aquifer, USA—Groundwater development and sustainability, *in* Hiscock, K.M., Rivett, M.O., and Davison, R.M., eds., Sustainable groundwater development: London, Geological Society Special Publication 193, p. 99–119.

DePaul, V.T., Rice, D.E., and Zapecza, O.S., 2008, Water-level changes in aquifers of the Atlantic Coastal Plain, predevelopment to 2000: U.S. Geological Survey Scientific Investigations Report 2007–5247, 88 p.

DePaul, V.T., Rosman, Robert, and Lacombe, P.J., 2009, Water-level conditions in selected confined aquifers of the New Jersey and Delaware coastal plain, 2003: U.S. Geological Survey Scientific Investigations Report 2008–5145, 123 p., 9 pls.

Dial, D.C., and Sumner, D.M., 1989, Geohydrology and simulated effects of pumpage on the New Orleans aquifer system at New Orleans, Louisiana: Louisiana Department of Transportation and Development Water Resources Technical Report 46, 54 p.

Dial, D.C., and Tomaszewski, D.J., 1988, Geohydrology, water quality, and effects of pumpage on the New Orleans aquifer system, northern Jefferson Parish, Louisiana: U.S. Geological Survey Water-Resources Investigations Report 88–4097, 34 p.

Dugan, J.T., and Zelt, R.B., 2000, Simulation and analysis of soil-water conditions in the Great Plains and adjacent areas, central United States, 1951–80: U.S. Geological Survey Water-Supply Paper 2427, 81 p.

Duxbury, A.C., Duxbury, A.B., and Sverdrup, K.A., 2000, An introduction to the world's oceans (6th ed.): McGraw-Hill, Boston, 528 p.

Eaton, T.T., Hart, D.J., Bradbury, K.R., and Wang, H.F., 2000, Appendix B—Hydraulic conductivity and specific storage of the Maquoketa shale: University of Wisconsin – Water Resources Institute, WGNHS Open-File Report 2000–01, 39 p.

Emery, P.A., 1979, Geohydrology of the San Luis Valley, Colorado, USA, in The hydrology of areas of low precipitation; Proceedings of the Canberra Symposium, December 1979: IAHS Publication 128, p. 297–305.

Emery, P.A., Patten, E.P., Jr., and Moore, J.E., 1975, Analog model study of the hydrology of the San Luis Valley, south-central Colorado: Denver, Colo., Colorado Water Conservation Board, Water Resources Circular 29, 21 p.

Eychaner, J.H., 1983, Geohydrology and effects of water use in the Black Mesa area, Navajo and Hopi Indian Reservations, Arizona: U.S. Geological Survey Water-Supply Paper 2201, 26 p.

Famiglietti, J.S., Lo, M., Ho, S.L., Bethune, J., Anderson, K.J., Syed, T.H., Swenson, S.C., de Linage, C.R., and Rodell, M., 2011, Satellites measure recent rates of groundwater depletion in California's Central Valley: Geophysical Research Letters, v. 38, L03403, doi:10.1029/2010GL046442.

Fanning, J.L., 1999, Water use in coastal Georgia by county and source, 1997, and water-use trends, 1980–97: Georgia Geologic Survey Informational Circular 104, 37 p.

Faunt, C.C., Belitz, Kenneth, and Hanson, R.T., 2009a, Chapter B—Groundwater availability in California's Central Valley, in Faunt, C.C., ed., Groundwater availability of the Central Valley Aquifer, California: U.S. Geological Survey Professional Paper 1766, p. 59–120.

Faunt, C.C., Hanson, R.T., Belitz, Kenneth, Schmid, Wolfgang, Predmore, S.P., Rewis, D.L., and McPherson, Kelly, 2009b, Chapter C—Numerical model of the hydrologic landscape and groundwater flow in California's Central Valley, in Faunt, C.C., ed., Groundwater availability of the Central Valley Aquifer, California: U.S. Geological Survey Professional Paper 1766, p. 121–212.

Faunt, C.C., D'Agnese, F.A., and O'Brien, G.M., 2010a, Hydrology, in Belcher, W.R. and Sweetkind, D.S., eds., Death Valley regional groundwater flow system, Nevada and California—Hydrogeologic framework and transient groundwater flow model: U.S. Geological Survey Professional Paper 1711, chap. D, p. 137–159.

Faunt, C.C., Blainey, J.B., Hill, M.C., D'Agnese, F.A., and O'Brien, G.M., 2010b, Transient numerical model, in Belcher, W.R. and Sweetkind, D.S., eds., Death Valley regional groundwater flow system, Nevada and California—Hydrogeologic framework and transient groundwater flow model: U.S. Geological Survey Professional Paper 1711, chap. F, p. 257–344.

Feinstein, D.T., Hart, D.J., and Krohelski, J.T., 2004, The value of long-term monitoring in the development of ground-water-flow models: U.S. Geological Survey Fact Sheet 116–03, 4 p.

Fleck, W.B., and Vroblesky, D.A., 1996, Simulation of ground-water flow of the coastal plain aquifers in parts of Maryland, Delaware, and the District of Columbia: U.S. Geological Survey Professional Paper 1404–J, 41 p.

Franke, O.L., and McClymonds, N.E., 1972, Summary of the hydrologic situation on Long Island, New York, as a guide to water-management alternatives: U.S. Geological Survey Professional Paper 627–F, 59 p.

Freihoefer, A., Mason, D., Jahnke, P., Dubas, L., and Hutchinson, K., 2009, Regional groundwater flow model of the Salt River Valley, Phoenix Active Management Area, Model update and calibration: Arizona Department of Water Resources, Modeling Report no. 19, 194 p., accessed February 11, 2011, at *http://www.adwr.state.az.us/azdwr/ Hydrology/Modeling/documents/SRV8306_Model_Report. pdf*.

Frenzel, P.F., 1992, Simulation of ground-water flow in the Mesilla Basin, Doña Ana County, New Mexico, and El Paso County, Texas—Supplement to Open-File Report 88–305: U.S. Geological Survey Water-Resources Investigations Report 91–4155, 152 p.

Frenzel, P.F., and Kaehler, C.A., 1992, Geohydrology and simulation of ground-water flow in the Mesilla Basin, Doña Ana County, New Mexico, and El Paso County, Texas: U.S. Geological Survey Professional Paper 1407–C, 105 p.

Galloway, D.L., Alley, W.M., Barlow, P.M., Reilly, T.E., and Tucci, Patrick, 2003, Evolving issues and practices in managing ground-water resources—Case studies on the role of science: U.S. Geological Survey Circular 1247, 73 p.

Galloway, D.L., Jones, D.R., and Ingebritsen, S.E., eds., 1999, Land subsidence in the United States: U.S. Geological Survey Circular 1182, 177 p.

Garabedian, S.P., 1992, Hydrology and digital simulation of the regional aquifer system, eastern Snake River Plain, Idaho: U.S. Geological Survey Professional Paper 1408–F, 65 p.

Gaum, C.H., 1953, High Plains, or Llano Estacado, Texas-New Mexico, *in* The physical and economic foundation of natural resources, IV, Subsurface facilities of water management and patterns of supply—Type area studies: Interior and Insular Affairs Committee, House of Representatives, United States Congress, Chapter 6, p. 94–104.

Gellici, J.A., and Lautier, J.C., 2010, Chapter B—Hydrogeologic framework of the Atlantic Coastal Plain, North and South Carolina, *in* Campbell, B.G., and Coes, A.L., eds., Groundwater availability in the Atlantic Coastal Plain of North and South Carolina: U.S. Geological Survey Professional Paper 1773, p. 49–162.

Giese, G.L., Eimers, J.L., and Coble, R.W., 1991, Simulation of ground-water flow in the coastal plain aquifer system of North Carolina: U.S. Geological Survey Open-File Report 90–372, 178 p.

Goodell, S.A., 1988, Water use on the Snake River Plain, Idaho and eastern Oregon: U.S. Geological Survey Professional Paper 1408–E, 51 p.

Groschen, G.E., 1985, Simulated effects of projected pumping on the availability of freshwater in the Evangeline aquifer in an area southwest of Corpus Christi, Texas: U.S. Geological Survey Water-Resources Investigations Report 85–4182, 103 p.

Groschen, G.E., 1994, Simulation of ground-water flow and the movement of saline water in the Hueco Bolson aquifer, El Paso, Texas, and adjacent areas: U.S. Geological Survey Open-File Report 92–171, 87 p.

Grubb, H.F., 1986, Gulf Coast regional aquifer-system analysis—a Mississippi perspective: U.S. Geological Survey Water-Resources Investigations Report 86–4162, 22 p.

Grubb, H.F., 1998, Summary of hydrology of the regional aquifer systems, Gulf Coastal Plain, south-central United States: U.S. Geological Survey Professional Paper 1416–A, 61 p.

Guo, Weixing, and Langevin, C.D., 2002, User's guide to SEAWAT—A computer program for simulation of three-dimensional variable-density ground-water flow: U.S. Geological Survey Techniques of Water-Resources Investigations, book 6, chap. A7, 77 p.

Gutentag, E.D., Heimes, F.J., Krothe, N.C., Luckey, R.R., and Weeks, J.B., 1984, Geohydrology of the High Plains aquifer in parts of Colorado, Kansas, Nebraska, New Mexico, Oklahoma, South Dakota, Texas, and Wyoming: U.S. Geological Survey Professional Paper 1400–B, 63 p.

Hansen, A.J., Jr., Vaccaro, J.J., and Bauer, H.H., 1994, Ground-water flow simulation of the Columbia Plateau regional aquifer system, Washington, Oregon, and Idaho: U.S. Geological Survey Water-Resources Investigations Report 91–4187, 81 p.

Hansen, H.J., 1977, Geologic and hydrologic data from two core holes drilled through the Aquia Formation (Eocene-Paleocene) in Prince George's and Queen Anne's Counties, Maryland: Maryland Geological Survey Open-File Report 77-02-1, 77 p.

Hanson, R.T., McLean, J.S., and Miller, R.S., 1994, Hydrogeologic framework and preliminary simulation of ground-water flow in the Mimbres Basin, southwestern New Mexico: U.S. Geological Survey Water-Resources Investigations Report 94–4011, 118 p.

Harbaugh, A.W., 2005, MODFLOW-2005, The U.S. Geological Survey modular ground-water model—The ground-water flow process: U.S. Geological Survey Techniques and Methods, book 6, chap. A16, variously paged.

Harbaugh, A.W., and McDonald, M.G., 1996, User's documentation for MODFLOW-96, an update to the U.S. Geological Survey modular finite-difference ground-water flow model: U.S. Geological Survey Open-File Report 96–485, 56 p.

Harbaugh, A.W., Banta, E.R., Hill, M.C., and McDonald, M.G., 2000, MODFLOW-2000, The U.S. Geological Survey modular ground-water model—User guide to modularization concepts and the ground-water flow process: U.S. Geological Survey Open-File Report 00–92, 121 p.

Harrill, J.R., 1976, Pumping and depletion of ground-water storage in Las Vegas Valley, Nevada, 1955–74: Nevada Division of Water Resources, Water Resources Bulletin 44, 70 p.

Harsh, J.F., and Laczniak, R.J., 1990, Conceptualization and analysis of the ground-water flow system in the coastal plain of Virginia and adjacent parts of Maryland and North Carolina: U.S. Geological Survey Professional Paper 1404–F, 100 p.

Hart, R.J., and Sottilare, J.P., 1988, Progress report on the ground-water, surface-water, and quality-of-water monitoring program, Black Mesa area, northeastern Arizona—1987–88: U.S. Geological Survey Open-File Report 88–467, 27 p.

Hart, R.J., and Sottilare, J.P., 1989, Progress report on the ground-water, surface-water, and quality-of-water monitoring program, Black Mesa area, northeastern Arizona—1988–89: U.S. Geological Survey Open-File Report 89–383, 33 p.

Hawley, J.W., Kennedy, J.F., and Creel, B.J., 2001, The Mesilla Basin aquifer system of New Mexico, West Texas, and Chihuahua—An overview of its hydrogeologic framework and related aspects of groundwater flow and chemistry, in R.E. Mace, W.F. Mullican III, and E.S. Angle, eds., Aquifers of West Texas, Texas Water Development Board Report 356, p. 76–99.

Healy, R.W., Winter, T.C., LaBaugh, J.W., and Franke, O.L., 2007, Water budgets—Foundations for effective water-resources and environmental management: U.S. Geological Survey Circular 1308, 90 p.

Hearne, G.A., and Dewey, J.D., 1988, Hydrologic analysis of the Rio Grande Basin north of Embudo, New Mexico; Colorado and New Mexico: U.S. Geological Survey Water-Resources Investigations Report 86–4113, 244 p.

Heimlich, R.E., Wiebe, K.D., Claassen, R., Gadsby, D., and House, R.M., 1998, Wetlands and agriculture—Private interests and public benefits: Resource Economics Division, Economic Research Service, U.S. Department of Agriculture, Agricultural Economic Report No. 765, 94 p.

Helgesen, J.O., Jorgensen, D.G., Leonard, R.B., and Signor, D.C., 1984, Regional study of the Dakota aquifer, Darton's Dakota revisited. in Jorgensen, D.G., and Signor, D.C., eds., Geohydrology of the Dakota aquifer—Proceedings of the First C.V. Theis Conference on Geohydrology: Worthington, Ohio, National Water Well Association, p. 69–73.

Heywood, C.E., and Pope, J.P., 2009, Simulation of ground-water flow in the Coastal Plain aquifer system of Virginia: U.S. Geological Survey Scientific Investigations Report 2009–5039, 115 p.

Heywood, C.E., and Yager, R.M., 2003, Simulated ground-water flow in the Hueco Bolson, an alluvial-basin aquifer system near El Paso, Texas: Water-Resources Investigations Report 02–4108, 73 p.

High Plains Underground Water Conservation District No. 1, 2010, The Ogallala Aquifer, accessed November 2010 at *http://www.hpwd.com/the_ogallala.asp.*

Hill, M.C., and Tiedeman, C.R., 2007, Effective groundwater model calibration; with analysis of data, sensitivities, predictions, and uncertainty: New York, Wiley, 455 p.

Hillhouse, J.W., Reichard, E.G., and Ponti, D.J., 2002, Probing the Los Angeles Basin—Insights into ground-water resources and earthquake hazards: U.S. Geological Survey Fact Sheet 086–02, 2 p.

Holmes, W.F., and Thiros, S.A., 1990, Ground-water hydrology of the Pahvant Valley and adjacent areas, Utah: State of Utah, Department of Natural Resources, Technical Publication No. 98, 64 p.

Hood, J.W., and Knowles, D.B., 1952, Summary of ground-water development in the Pecos area, Reeves and Ward Counties, Texas, 1947–51: Texas Board of Water Engineers Bulletin 5202, 11 p.

Huff, G.F., 2005, Simulation of ground-water flow in the basin-fill aquifer of the Tularosa Basin, south-central New Mexico, predevelopment through 2040: U.S. Geological Survey Scientific Investigations Report 2004–5197, 98 p.

Hunt, C.D., Jr., 1996, Geohydrology of the Island of Oahu, Hawaii: U.S. Geological Survey Professional Paper 1412–B, p. B19–B21.

Hutson, S.S., Barber, N.L., Kenny, J.F., Linsey, K.S., Lumia, D.S., and Maupin, M.A., 2004, Estimated use of water in the United States in 2000: U.S. Geological Survey Circular 1268, 46 p.

Ikehara, M.E., and Phillips, S.P., 1994, Determination of land subsidence related to ground-water-level declines using Global Positioning System and leveling surveys in Antelope Valley, Los Angeles and Kern Counties, California, 1992: U.S. Geological Survey Water-Resources Investigations Report 94–4184, 101 p.

Ireland, R.L., Poland, J.F., and Riley, F.S., 1984, Land subsidence in the San Joaquin Valley, California, as of 1980: U.S. Geological Survey Professional Paper 437–I, 93 p.

Johnson, T.A., and Chong, B., 2005, A century of groundwater changes in the Central and West Coast Basins: Water Replenishment District of Southern California Technical Bulletin v. 4.

Jones, I.C., 2001, Cenozoic Pecos alluvium aquifer, in Aquifers of West Texas by R.E. Mace and others: Texas Water Development Board Report 356, 263 p.

Jorgensen, D.G., and Signor, D.C., eds., 1984, Geohydrology of the Dakota aquifer—Proceedings of the First C.V. Theis Conference on Geohydrology: Worthington, Ohio, National Water Well Association, 247 p.

Kahle, S.C., Morgan, D.S., Welch, W.B., Ely, D.M., Hinkle, S.R., Vaccaro, J.J., and Orzol, L.L., 2011, Hydrogeologic framework and hydrologic budget components of the Columbia Plateau Regional Aquifer System, Washington, Oregon, and Idaho: U.S. Geological Survey Scientific Investigations Report 2011–5124, 66 p.

Kasmarek, M.C., and Robinson, J.L., 2004, Hydrogeology and simulation of ground-water flow and land-surface subsidence in the northern part of the Gulf Coast aquifer system, Texas: U.S. Geological Survey Scientific Investigations Report 2004–5102, 103 p.

Kasmarek, M.C., and Strom, E.W., 2002, Hydrogeology and simulation of ground-water flow and land-surface subsidence in the Chicot and Evangeline aquifers, Houston area, Texas: U.S. Geological Survey Water-Resources Investigations Report 02–4022, 61 p.

Kjelstrom, L.C., 1995, Streamflow gains and losses in the Snake River and ground-water budgets for the Snake River Plain, Idaho and eastern Oregon: U.S. Geological Survey Professional Paper 1408–C, 47 p.

Klemt, W.B., Duffin, G.L., and Elder, G.R., 1976, Ground-water resources of the Carrizo aquifer in the Winter Garden area of Texas, Volume 1: Texas Water Development Board Report 210, 30 p.

Konikow, L.F., 2011, Contribution of global groundwater depletion since 1900 to sea-level rise: Geophysical Research Letters, v. 38, L17401, doi:10.1029/2011GL048604.

Konikow, L.F., and Kendy, Eloise, 2005, Groundwater depletion—A global problem: Hydrogeology Journal, v. 13, no. 1, p. 317–320.

Konikow, L.F., and Neuzil, C.E., 2007, A method to estimate groundwater depletion from confining layers: Water Resources Research, v. 43, W07417, doi:10.1029/2006WR005597.

Krause, R.E., and Randolph, R.B., 1989, Hydrology of the Floridan aquifer system in southeast Georgia and adjacent parts of Florida and South Carolina: U.S. Geological Survey Professional Paper 1403–D, 65 p.

Lacombe, P.J., and Rosman, Robert, 2001, Water levels in, extent of freshwater in, and water withdrawals from ten confined aquifers, New Jersey and Delaware coastal plain, 1998: U.S. Geological Survey Water-Resources Investigations Report 00–4143, 10 over-size sheets.

Lautier, J.C., 2001, Hydrogeologic framework and ground water conditions in the North Carolina central coastal plain: North Carolina Department of Environment and Natural Resources, Division of Water Resources, 38 p.

Leahy, P.P., 1982, A three-dimensional ground-water-flow model modified to reduce computer-memory requirements and better simulate confining-bed and aquifer pinchouts: U.S. Geological Survey Water-Resources Investigations Report 82–4023, 59 p.

Leake, S.A., and Prudic, D.E., 1991, Documentation of a computer program to simulate aquifer-system compaction using the modular finite-difference ground-water flow model: U.S. Geological Survey Techniques of Water-Resources Investigations, book 6, chap. A2, 68 p.

Leake, S.A., Konieczki, A.D., and Rees, J.A.H., 2000, Desert basins of the Southwest: U.S. Geological Survey Fact Sheet 086–00, 4 p.

Leighton, D.A., and Phillips, S.P., 2003, Simulation of ground-water flow and land subsidence in the Antelope Valley ground-water basin, California: U.S. Geological Survey Water-Resources Investigations Report 03–4016, 107 p.

LeRoux, E.F., and Hamilton, L.J., 1985, South Dakota ground-water resources, in U.S. Geological Survey, eds., National water summary 1984; hydrologic events, selected water-quality trends, and ground-water resources: U.S. Geological Survey Water-Supply Paper 2275, p. 385–390.

Lohman, S.W., 1972, Ground-water hydraulics: U.S. Geological Survey Professional Paper 708, 70 p.

Lowry, M.E., Crist, M.A., and Tilstra, J.R., 1967, Geology and ground-water resources of Laramie County, Wyoming, with a section on Chemical quality of ground water and of surface water: U.S. Geological Survey Water-Supply Paper 1834, 71 p.

Luckey, R.R., Gutentag, E.D., and Weeks, J.B., 1981, Water-level and saturated-thickness changes, predevelopment to 1980, in the High Plains aquifer in parts of Colorado, Kansas, Nebraska, New Mexico, Oklahoma, South Dakota, Texas, and Wyoming: U.S. Geological Survey Hydrologic Atlas HA–652, 2 sheets, scale 1:2,500,000.

Mahon, G.L., and Ludwig, A.H., 1990, Simulation of ground-water flow in the Mississippi River Valley alluvial aquifer in eastern Arkansas: U.S. Geological Survey Water-Resources Investigations Report 89–4145, 57 p.

Mandle, R.J., and Kontis, A.L., 1992, Simulation of regional ground-water flow in the Cambrian-Ordovician aquifer system in the northern Midwest, United States: U.S. Geological Survey Professional Paper 1405–C, 97 p.

Martin, Angel, Jr., and Whiteman, C.D., Jr., 1989, Geohydrology and regional ground-water flow of the coastal lowlands aquifer system in parts of Louisiana, Mississippi, Alabama, and Florida—A preliminary analysis: U.S. Geological Survey Water-Resources Investigations Report 88–4100, 88 p.

Martin, Angel, Jr., and Whiteman, C.D., Jr., 1999, Hydrology of the coastal lowlands aquifer system in parts of Alabama, Florida, Louisiana, and Mississippi: U.S. Geological Survey Professional Paper 1416–H, 50 p., 8 pls.

Martin, Mary, 1998, Ground-water flow in the New Jersey coastal plain: U.S. Geological Survey Professional Paper 1404–H, 146 p.

Mason, J.L., 1998, Ground-water hydrology and simulated effects of development in the Milford area, an arid basin in southwestern Utah: U.S. Geological Survey Professional Paper 1409–G, 69 p., 2 pls.

McAda, D.P., and Barroll, Peggy, 2002, Simulation of groundwater flow in the Middle Rio Grande Basin between Cochiti and San Acacia, New Mexico: U.S. Geological Survey Water-Resources Investigations Report 02–4200, 81 p.

McCoy, T.W., 1991, Evaluation of the ground-water resources of the western portion of the Winter Garden area, Texas: Texas Water Development Board Report 334, 64 p.

McDonald, M.G., and Harbaugh, A.W., 1988, A modular three-dimensional finite difference ground-water flow model: U.S. Geological Survey Techniques of Water-Resources Investigations, book 6, chap. A1, 586 p.

McFarland, E.R., and Bruce, T.S., 2006, The Virginia coastal plain hydrogeologic framework: U.S. Geological Survey Professional Paper 1731, 118 p., 25 pls.

McGuire, V.L., 2001, Water-level changes in the High Plains aquifer, 1980 to 1999: U.S. Geological Survey Fact Sheet 029–01, 2 p.

McGuire, V.L., 2003, Water-level changes in the High Plains aquifer, predevelopment to 2001, 1999 to 2000, and 2000 to 2001: U.S. Geological Survey Fact Sheet FS–078–03, 4 p.

McGuire, V.L., 2004, Water-level changes in the High Plains aquifer, predevelopment to 2003 and 2002 to 2003: U.S. Geological Survey Fact Sheet 2004–3097, 6 p.

McGuire, V.L., 2007, Water-level changes in the High Plains aquifer, predevelopment to 2005 and 2003 to 2005: U.S. Geological Survey Scientific Investigations Report 2006–5324, 7 p.

McGuire, V.L., 2009, Water-level changes in the High Plains aquifer, predevelopment to 2007, 2005–06, and 2006–07: U.S. Geological Survey Scientific Investigations Report 2009–5019, 9 p.

McGuire, V.L., 2011, Water-level changes in the High Plains aquifer, predevelopment to 2009, 2007–08, and 2008–09, and change in water in storage, predevelopment to 2009: U.S. Geological Survey Scientific Investigations Report 2011–5089, 13 p. [revised December 2011].

McGuire, V.L., Johnson, M.R., Schieffer, R.L., Stanton, J.S., Sebree, S.K., and Verstraeten, I.M., 2003, Water in storage and approaches to ground-water management, High Plains aquifer, 2000: U.S. Geological Survey Circular 1243, 51 p.

McLean, J.S., 1970, Saline ground-water resources of the Tularosa Basin, New Mexico: U.S. Department of the Interior Office of Saline Water Research and Development Progress Report 561, 128 p.

Meinzer, O.E., and Hare, R.F., 1915, Geology and water resources of Tularosa Basin, New Mexico: U.S. Geological Survey Water-Supply Paper 343, 317 p., 19 pls.

Mendenhall, W.C., 1905a, Development of underground waters in the central coastal plain region of southern California: U.S. Geological Survey Water-Supply Paper 138, 162 p.

Mendenhall, W.C., 1905b, Development of underground waters in the western coastal plain region of southern California: U.S. Geological Survey Water-Supply Paper 139, 103 p.

Meng, A.A., III, and Harsh, J.F., 1988, Hydrogeologic framework of the Virginia coastal plain: U.S. Geological Survey Professional Paper 1404–C, 82 p.

Menking, K.M., Syed, K.H., Anderson, R.Y., Shafike, N.G., and Arnold, J.G., 2003, Model estimates of runoff in the closed, semiarid Estancia basin, central New Mexico, USA: Hydrological Sciences, v. 48, no. 6, p. 953–970.

Meyer, W.R., and Carr, J.E., 1979, A digital model for simulation of ground-water hydrology in the Houston area, Texas: Texas Department of Water Resources Limited Publication LP–103, 133 p.

Miller, J.A., 1986, Hydrogeologic framework of the Floridan aquifer system in Florida and in parts of Georgia, Alabama, and South Carolina: U.S. Geological Survey Professional Paper 1403–B, 91 p., 33 pls.

Misut, P.E., and Monti, Jack, Jr., 1999, Simulation of groundwater flow and pumpage in Kings and Queens Counties, Long Island, New York, U.S. Geological Survey Water-Resources Investigations Report 98–4071, 50 p.

Monti, Jack, Jr., Busciolano, R.J., and Terracciano, S.A., 2008, Monitoring ground-water levels, Long Island, NY [abs.], in Sixth National Monitoring Conference–Monitoring—Key to Understanding Our Waters, May 18–22, 2008: Atlantic City, N.J., Water Environment Federation.

Moore, J.E., Raynolds, R.G., and Barkmann, P.E., 2004, Groundwater mining of bedrock aquifers in the Denver Basin—Past, present, and future: Environmental Geology, v. 47, p. 63–68, doi 10.1007/s00254-004-1127-8.

Moreo, M.T., Halford, K.J., La Camera, R.J., and Laczniak, R.J., 2003, Estimated ground-water withdrawals from the Death Valley regional flow system, Nevada and California, 1913–98: U.S. Geological Survey Water-Resources Investigations Report 03–4245, 28 p.

Morgan, D.S., and Dettinger, M.D., 1996, Ground-water conditions in Las Vegas Valley, Clark County, Nevada; Part 2, Hydrogeology and simulation of ground-water flow: U.S. Geological Survey Water-Supply Paper 2320–B, 124 p.

Mower, R.W., 1964, Pavant Valley, in Developing a state water plan, ground-water conditions in Utah, Spring of 1964, by Ted Arnow and others: Utah Water and Power Board, Cooperative Investigations Report Number 2, 104 p.

Mower, R.W., 1965, Ground-water resources of Pavant Valley, Utah: U.S. Geological Survey Water-Supply Paper 1794, 78 p.

Mower, R.W., 1982, Hydrology of the Beryl-Enterprise area, Escalante Desert, Utah, with emphasis on ground water: Utah Department of Natural Resources Technical Publication No. 73, 66 p.

Mower, R.W., and Cordova, R.M., 1974, Water resources of the Milford area, Utah, with emphasis on ground water: State of Utah Department of Natural Resources Technical Publication No. 43, 106 p.

Muller, D.A., and Price, R.D., 1979, Ground-water availability in Texas, estimates and projections through 2030: Texas Department of Water Resources Report 238, 77 p.

Newton, G.D., 1991, Geohydrology of the regional aquifer system, western Snake River Plain, southwestern Idaho: U.S. Geological Survey Professional Paper 1408–G, 52 p.

Nichols, W.D., Shade, P.J., and Hunt, C.D., Jr., 1996, Summary of the Oahu, Hawaii, Regional Aquifer-System Analysis: U.S. Geological Survey Professional Paper 1412–A, 71 p.

Ogilbee, W., Wesselman, J.B., and Ireland, B., 1962, Geology and ground-water resources of Reeves County, Texas: Texas Water Commission Bulletin 6214, v. 1 and 2, 435 p.

Oki, D.S., 1998, Geohydrology of the Central Oahu, Hawaii, ground-water flow systems and numerical simulation of the effects of additional pumping: U.S. Geological Survey Water-Resources Investigations Report 97–4276, 132 p.

Oki, D.S., 2005, Numerical simulation of the effects of low-permeability valley-fill barriers and the redistribution of ground-water withdrawals in the Pearl Harbor area, Oahu, Hawaii: U.S. Geological Survey Scientific Investigations Report 2005–5253, 111 p.

Oki, D.S., Gingerich, S.B., and Whitehead, R.L., 1999, Hawaii, in Ground water atlas of the United States, Segment 13, Alaska, Hawaii, Puerto Rico, and the U.S. Virgin Islands: U.S. Geological Survey Hydrologic Investigation Atlas 730–N, p. N12–N22.

Olcott, P.G., 1995, Ground water atlas of the United States, Segment 12, Connecticut, Maine, Massachusetts, New Hampshire, New York, Rhode Island, Vermont: U.S. Geological Survey Hydrologic Investigations Atlas 730–M, 28 p.

Orr, B.R., 1997, Geohydrology of the Idaho National Engineering and Environmental Laboratory, Eastern Snake River Plain, Idaho: U.S. Geological Survey Fact Sheet 130–97, 4 p.

Orr, B.R., and Myers, R.G., 1986, Water resources in basin-fill deposits in the Tularosa Basin, New Mexico: U.S. Geological Survey Water-Resources Investigations Report 85–4219, 94 p.

Page, R.W., 1986, Geology of the fresh ground-water basin of the Central Valley, California, with texture maps and sections: U.S. Geological Survey Professional Paper 1401–C, 54 p.

Paschke, S.S., Banta, E.R., and Litke, D.W., 2011a, Effects of development on groundwater availability of the Denver Basin aquifer system, Colorado, in Paschke, S.S., ed., Groundwater availability of the Denver Basin aquifer system, Colorado: U.S. Geological Survey Professional Paper 1770, chap. B, p. 95–180.

Paschke, S.S., Banta, E.R., Dupree, J.A., and Capesius, J.P., 2011b, Introduction, conceptual model, hydrogeologic framework, and predevelopment groundwater availability of the Denver Basin aquifer system, Colorado, in Paschke, S.S., ed., Groundwater availability of the Denver Basin aquifer system, Colorado: U.S. Geological Survey Professional Paper 1770, chap. A, p. 1–93.

Pavelis, G.A., ed., 1987, Farm drainage in the U.S.—History, status, and prospects: Economic Research Service, U.S. Department of Agriculture, Miscellaneous Publication No. 1455, 170 p.

Pavelko, M.T., Wood, D.B., and Laczniak, R.J., 1999, Las Vegas, Nevada: in Galloway, D.L., Jones, D.R., and Ingebritsen, S.E., eds., Land subsidence in the United States: U.S. Geological Survey Circular 1182, p. 49–64.

Payne, D.F., 2010, Effects of sea-level rise and pumpage elimination on saltwater intrusion in the Hilton Head Island area, South Carolina, 2004–2104: U.S. Geological Survey Scientific Investigations Report 2009–5251, 83 p.

Payne, D.F., Rumman, M.A., and Clarke, J.S., 2005, Simulation of ground-water flow in coastal Georgia and adjacent parts of South Carolina and Florida—Predevelopment, 1980, and 2000: U.S. Geological Survey Scientific Investigations Report 2005–5089, 82 p.

Peck, M.F., Clarke, J.S., Ransom, C., III, and Richards, C.J., 1999, Potentiometric surface of the upper Floridan Aquifer in Georgia and adjacent parts of Alabama, Florida, and South Carolina, May 1998, and water-level trends in Georgia, 1900–98: Georgia Geologic Survey Hydrologic Atlas 22, 1 sheet.

Petkewich, M.D., and Campbell, B.G., 2007, Hydrogeology and simulation of ground-water flow near Mount Pleasant, South Carolina—Predevelopment, 2004, and predicted scenarios for 2030: U.S. Geological Survey Scientific Investigations Report 2007–5126, 79 p.

Plume, R.W., 1989, Ground-water conditions in Las Vegas Valley, Clark County, Nevada—Part I, Hydrogeologic framework: U.S. Geological Survey Water-Supply Paper 2320–A, 15 p.

Poland, J.F., Garrett, A.A., and Sinnott, Allen, 1959, Geology, hydrology, and chemical character of ground waters in the Torrance-Santa Monica area, California: U.S. Geological Survey Water-Supply Paper 1461, 425 p., 21 pls.

Pope, J.P., and Burbey, T.J., 2004, Multiple-aquifer characterization from single borehole extensometer records: Ground Water, v. 42, no. 1, p. 45–58.

Prudic, D.E., and Herman, M.E., 1996, Ground-water flow and simulated effects of development in Paradise Valley, a basin tributary to the Humboldt River in Humboldt County, Nevada: U.S. Geological Survey Professional Paper 1409–F, 92 p.

Reichard, E.G., and Meadows, J.K., 1992, Evaluation of a ground-water flow and transport model of the upper Coachella Valley, California: U.S. Geological Survey Water-Resources Investigations Report 91–4142, 101 p.

Reichard, E.G., Land, Michael, Crawford, S.M., Johnson, Tyler, Everett, R.R., Kulshan, T.V., Ponti, D.J., Halford, K.J., Johnson, T.A., Paybins, K.S., and Nishikawa, Tracy, 2003, Geohydrology, geochemistry, and ground-water simulation-optimization of the Central and West Coast Basins, Los Angeles County, California: U.S. Geological Survey Water-Resources Investigations Report 03–4065, 184 p.

Robson, S.G., 1989, Alluvial and bedrock aquifers of the Denver Basin—Eastern Colorado's dual ground-water resource: U.S. Geological Survey Water-Supply Paper 2302, 40 p.

Roe, H.B., and Ayers, Q.C., 1954, Engineering for agricultural drainage: New York, McGraw-Hill, 501 p.

Rotzoll, Kolja, Oki, D.S., and El-Kadi, A.I., 2010, Changes of freshwater-lens thickness in basaltic island aquifers overlain by thick coastal sediments: Hydrogeology Journal, v. 18, p. 1425–1436, doi 10.1007/s10040-010-0602-4.

Ryder, P.D., 1996, Ground water atlas of the United States—Segment 4, Oklahoma Texas: U.S. Geological Survey Hydrologic Investigations Atlas 730–E, 30 p.

Ryder, P.D., and Ardis, A.F., 2002, Hydrology of the Texas Gulf Coast aquifer systems: U.S. Geological Survey Professional Paper 1416–E, 77 p.

Sandberg, G.W., 1964, Developing a state water plan, groundwater conditions in Utah, spring of 1964—Escalante Valley, Beryl-Enterprise District: Utah Water and Power Board Cooperative Investigations Report No. 2, 104 p.

Sanderson, Marie, 1993, Prevailing trade winds—Weather and climate in Hawai'i: Honolulu, University of Hawai'i Press, 126 p.

San Juan, C.A., Belcher, W.R., Laczniak, R.J., and Putnam, H.M., 2010, Hydrologic components for model development, in Belcher, W.R., and Sweetkind, D.S., eds., Death Valley regional groundwater flow system, Nevada and California—Hydrogeologic framework and transient groundwater flow model: U.S. Geological Survey Professional Paper 1711, chap. C, p. 95–132.

Scheiderer, R.M., and Freiwald, D.A., 2006, Monitoring the recovery of the Sparta aquifer in southern Arkansas and northern Louisiana: U.S. Geological Survey Fact Sheet 2006–3090, 4 p.

Schmid, Wolfgang, Hanson, R.T., Maddock, Thomas, III, and Leake, S.A., 2006, User guide for the Farm Process (FMP1) for the U.S. Geological Survey's modular three-dimensional finite-difference ground-water flow model, MODFLOW-2000: U.S. Geological Survey Techniques and Methods, book 6, chap. A17, 127 p.

Schrader, T.P., 2001, Status of water levels and selected water-quality conditions in the Mississippi River valley alluvial aquifer in eastern Arkansas, 2000: U.S. Geological Survey Water-Resources Investigations Report 01–4124, 52 p.

Schwartz, F.W., and Ibaraki, Motomu, 2011, Groundwater—A resource in decline: Elements, v. 7, p. 175–179, doi 10.2113/gselements.7.3.175.

Scorca, M.P., and Monti, Jack, Jr., 2001, Estimates of nitrogen loads entering Long Island Sound from ground water and streams on Long Island, New York, 1985–96: U.S. Geological Survey Water-Resources Investigations Report 00–4196, 29 p.

Shafike, N.G., and Flanigan, K.G., 1999, Hydrologic modeling of the Estancia basin, New Mexico, *in* Pazzaglia, F.J., and Lucas, S.G., eds., Albuquerque geology: New Mexico Geological Society Guidebook, 50th Field Conference, p. 409–418.

Sheng, Z., Mace, R.E., and Fahy, M.P., 2001, Aquifers of West Texas: Texas Water Development Board Report 356, chap. 6, p. 66–75.

Slaugh, B.A., 2002, Escalante Valley, Milford area: *in* Ground-water conditions in Utah, spring 2002, by C.B. Burden and others: Utah Division of Water Resources Cooperative Investigations Report No. 43, 120 p.

Sneed, Michelle, 2010, Measurement of land subsidence using interferometry, Coachella Valley, California, *in* Carreón-Freyre, Dora, Cerca, Mariano, and Galloway, D.L., eds., Land subsidence, associated hazards and the role of natural resources development, Proceedings EISOLS 2010, Querétaro, Mexico, October 17–22, 2010: International Association of Hydrological Sciences Publication 339, p. 260–263.

Sneed, Michelle, Stork, S.V., and Ikehara, M.E., 2002, Detection and measurement of land subsidence using global positioning system and interferometric synthetic aperture radar, Coachella Valley, California, 1998–2000: U.S. Geological Survey Water-Resources Investigations Report 02–4239, 29 p.

Soeder, D.J., Raffensperger, J.P., and Nardi, M.R., 2007, Effects of withdrawals on ground-water levels in Southern Maryland and the adjacent Eastern Shore, 1980–2005: U.S. Geological Survey Scientific Investigations Report 2007–5249, 82 p.

Snyder, D.T., and Haynes, J.V., 2010, Groundwater conditions during 2009 and changes in groundwater levels from 1984 to 2009, Columbia Plateau Regional Aquifer System, Washington, Oregon, and Idaho: U.S. Geological Survey Scientific Investigations Report 2010–5040, 12 p.

Stamos, C.L., Cox, B.F., Izbicki, J.A., and Mendez, G.O., 2003, Geologic setting, geohydrology, and ground-water quality near the Helendale Fault in the Mojave River Basin, San Bernardino County, California: U.S. Geological Survey Water-Resources Investigations Report 03–4069, 44 p.

Stamos, C.L., Martin, Peter, Nishikawa, Tracy, and Cox, B.F., 2001a, Simulation of ground-water flow in the Mojave River basin, California: U.S. Geological Survey Water-Resources Investigations Report 01–4002, ver. 3, 128 p.

Stamos, C.L., Nishikawa, Tracy, and Martin, Peter, 2001b, Water supply in the Mojave River ground-water basin, 1931–99, and the benefits of artificial recharge: U.S. Geological Survey Fact Sheet 122–01, 4 p.

Strom, E.W., Houston, N.A., and Garcia, C.A., 2003, Selected hydrogeologic datasets for the Jasper aquifer, Texas: U.S. Geological Survey Open-File Report 03–299, 1 CD–ROM.

Swain, L.A., 1978, Predicted water-level and water-quality effects of artificial recharge in the upper Coachella Valley, California, using a finite-element digital model: U.S. Geological Survey Water-Resources Investigations Report 77–29, 54 p.

Sweetkind, D.S., Belcher, W.R., Faunt, C.C., and Potter, C.J., 2010, Geology and hydrogeology, *in* Belcher, W.R. and Sweetkind, D.S., eds., Death Valley regional ground-water flow system, Nevada and California—Hydrogeologic framework and transient groundwater flow model: U.S. Geological Survey Professional Paper 1711, chap. B, p. 19–94.

Swenson, R.L., 2002, Pahvant Valley, *in* Ground-water conditions in Utah, spring 2002, by C.B. Burden and others: Utah Division of Water Resources Cooperative Investigations Report No. 43, 120 p.

Takasaki, K.J., 1978, Summary appraisals of the Nation's ground-water resources—Hawaii region: U.S. Geological Survey Professional Paper 813–M, 29 p.

Takasaki, K.J., Hirashima, G.T., and Lubke, E.R., 1969, Water resources of windward Oahu, Hawaii: U.S. Geological Survey Water-Supply Paper 1894, 119 p.

Templin, W.E., Phillips, S.P., Cherry, D.E., DeBortoli, M.L., and others, 1995, Land use and water use in Antelope Valley, California: U.S. Geological Survey Water-Resources Investigations Report 94–4208, 97 p.

Texas Water Development Board, 2001, Surveys of irrigation in Texas, 1958, 1964, 1969, 1974, 1984, 1989, 1994, and 2000: Texas Water Development Board Report 347, 102 p.

Theis, C.V., 1940, The source of water derived from wells—Essential factors controlling the response of an aquifer to development: Civil Engineering, v. 10, p. 277–280.

Thomas, B.E., 2002, Ground-water, surface-water, and water-chemistry data, Black Mesa area, northeastern Arizona—2000–2001, and performance and sensitivity of the 1988 USGS numerical model of the N aquifer: U.S. Geological Survey Water-Resources Investigations Report 02–4211, 75 p.

Thomas, R.P., 2004, Estancia Basin dynamic water budget: Sandia National Laboratories, Albuquerque, N.M., Report SAND2004–1796, 19 p.

Tiedeman, C.R., Kernodle, J.M., and McAda, D.P., 1998, Application of nonlinear-regression methods to a groundwater flow model of the Albuquerque Basin, New Mexico: U.S. Geological Survey Water-Resources Investigations Report 98–4172, 90 p.

Tillman, F.D., and Leake, S.A., 2010, Trends in groundwater levels in wells in the active management areas of Arizona, USA: Hydrogeology Journal, v. 18, no. 6, p. 1515–1524, doi 10.1007/s10040-010-0603-3.

Tillman, F.D, Cordova, J.T., Leake, S.A., Thomas, B.E., and Callegary, J.B., 2011, Water availability and use pilot—Methods development for a regional assessment of groundwater availability, southwest alluvial basins, Arizona: U.S. Geological Survey Scientific Investigations Report 2011–5071, 118 p.

Trescott, P.C., 1975, Documentation of finite-difference model for simulation of three-dimensional ground-water flow: U.S. Geological Survey Open-File Report 75–438, 32 p.

Trescott, P.C., and Larson, S.P., 1976, Documentation of finite-difference model for simulation of three-dimensional ground-water flow, Supplement to Open-File Report 75–438: U. S. Geological Survey Open-File Report 76–591, 21 p.

Trescott, P.C., Pinder, G.F., and Larson, S.P., 1976, Finite-difference model for aquifer simulation in two dimensions with results of numerical experiments: U.S. Geological Survey Techniques of Water-Resources Investigations, book 7, chap. C1, 116 p.

Turco, M.J., 1999, Regional water-level changes for the Cambrian-Ordovician aquifer in Iowa, 1975 to 1997: U.S. Geological Survey Water-Resources Investigations Report 99–4134, 11 p.

Tyley, S.J., 1974, Analog model study of the ground-water basin of the upper Coachella Valley, California: U.S. Geological Survey Water-Supply Paper 2027, 77 p.

U.S. Geological Survey, 2002, Concepts for national assessment of water availability and use: U.S. Geological Survey Circular 1223, 34 p.

U.S. Geological Survey, 2008, Ground-water availability assessment for the Columbia Plateau Regional Aquifer System, Washington, Oregon, and Idaho: U.S. Geological Survey Fact Sheet 2008–3086, 2 p.

Vaccaro, J.J., 1999, Summary of the Columbia Plateau regional aquifer-system analysis, Washington, Oregon, and Idaho: U.S. Geological Survey Professional Paper 1413–A, 51 p.

Visocky, A.P., 1997, Water-level trends and pumpage in the deep bedrock aquifers in the Chicago region, 1991–1995: Illinois State Water Survey Circular 182, 45 p.

Water Replenishment District of Southern California, 2010, Engineering Survey and Report, 2010 [Version of May 11, 2010]: Lakewood, Calif., Water Replenishment District of Southern California, 77 p.

Waterstone Environmental Hydrology and Engineering, Inc., 2003, Groundwater availability of the Central Gulf Coast aquifer—Numerical simulations to 2050, Central Gulf Coast, Texas: Report submitted to Texas Water Development Board, 115 p., *http://www.twdb.state.tx.us/groundwater/models/gam/glfc_c/Waterstone_Conceptual_Report.pdf*.

Weeks, J.B., Gutentag, E.D., Heimes, F.J., and Luckey, R.R., 1988, Summary of the High Plains regional aquifer-system analysis in parts of Colorado, Kansas, Nebraska, New Mexico, Oklahoma, South Dakota, Texas, and Wyoming: U.S Geological Survey Professional Paper 1400–A, 30 p.

Weiss, J.S., and Williamson, A.K., 1985, Subdivision of thick sedimentary units into layers for simulation of ground-water flow: Ground Water, v. 23, no. 6, p. 767–774.

Wesselman, J.B., 1967, Ground-water resources of Jasper and Newton Counties, Texas: Texas Water Development Board Report 59, 177 p.

Wheeler, J.C., 1998, Freshwater use in Maryland, 1995: U.S. Geological Survey Fact Sheet 115–98, 1 sheet.

Wheeler, J.C., 1999, Freshwater use in Delaware, 1995: U.S. Geological Survey Fact Sheet 126–99, 1 sheet.

Wheeler, J.C., and Wilde, F.D., 1989, Ground-water use in the coastal plain of Maryland, 1900–1980: U.S. Geological Survey Open-File Report 87–540, 173 p.

Whitehead, R.L., 1992, Geohydrologic framework of the Snake River Plain regional aquifer system, Idaho and eastern Oregon: U.S. Geological Survey Professional Paper 1408–B, 32 p.

Whitehead, R.L., 1994, Ground water atlas of the United States; Segment 7, Idaho, Oregon, and Washington: U.S. Geological Survey Hydrologic Investigations Atlas 730–H, 31 p.

Williamson, A.K., and Grubb, H.F., 2001, Ground-water flow in the Gulf Coast aquifer systems, south-central United States: U.S. Geological Survey Professional Paper 1416–F, 173 p.

Williamson, A.K., Prudic, D.E., and Swain, L.A., 1989, Ground-water flow in the Central Valley, California: U.S. Geological Survey Professional Paper 1401–D, 127 p.

Wilson, B.C., and Lucero, A.A., 1997, Water use by categories in New Mexico counties and river basins, and irrigated acreage in 1995: Santa Fe, New Mexico State Engineer Office Technical Report 49, 149 p.

Winner, M.D., Jr., and Coble, R.W., 1996, Hydrogeologic framework of the North Carolina coastal plain: U.S. Geological Survey Professional Paper 1404–I, 106 p., 24 pls.

Wintz, W.A., Kazmann, R.G., and Smith, C.G., Jr., 1970, Subsidence and ground-water offtake in the Baton Rouge area: Louisiana Water Resources Research Institute Bulletin 6, 20 p.

Wood, D.B., 2000, Water use and associated effects on ground-water levels, Las Vegas Valley and vicinity, Clark County, Nevada, 1980–95: Nevada Division of Water Resources, Water-Resources Information Report 35, 101 p.

Young, H.L., 1992a, Summary of ground-water hydrology of the Cambrian-Ordovician aquifer system in the northern Midwest, United States: U.S. Geological Survey Professional Paper 1405–A, 55 p.

Young, H.L., 1992b, Hydrogeology of the Cambrian-Ordovician aquifer system in the northern Midwest, United States: U.S. Geological Survey Professional Paper 1405–B, 99 p.

Zapecza, O.S., 1989, Hydrogeologic framework of the New Jersey coastal plain: U.S. Geological Survey Professional Paper 1404–B, 49 p.

Zapecza, O.S., Voronin, L.M., and Martin, Mary, 1987, Ground-water withdrawal and water-level data used to simulate regional flow in the major coastal plain aquifers of New Jersey: U.S. Geological Survey Water-Resources Investigations 87–4038, 120 p., 10 pls.